SHIPWRECKS NEAR BARNEGAT INLET

LONG BEACH ISLAND

•

Second Edition

•

David J. Seibold   Charles J. Adams III

EXETER HOUSE BOOKS
1995

SHIPWRECKS NEAR BARNEGAT INLET

by David J. Seibold and Charles J. Adams III

©2008

Exeter House Books
PO Box 6411
Wyomissing, PA 19610
www.ExeterHouseBooks.com

ISBN 978-1-880683-04-0
First Printing, 1984

Printed in the United States of America

TABLE OF CONTENTS

Foreword to the 1984 First Edition.................... 1
Introduction to the 1984 First Edition.................3
Introduction to the 1995 Second Edition............. 7
The Death of a "Double-Ender"........................8
Shreds of Evidence................................... 10
Down With His Ship.................................. 12
The Pie-Eyed Pilot and the Wreck of the Magnus.............. 14
A Shocking Arrival....................................16
Life-Savers to the Rescue.............................19
Heroics, Survival, and Death......................... 23
The "Wendt" Washes Ashore.........................26
Inferno At Sea..28
The Ship of Death.....................................32
Beneath the Shifting Sands........................... 35
The Bone Wreck.......................................38
The Gales of December............................... 41
The Killer Wave.......................................45
The Mystery of the Cedar Creek Wreck............. 48
The Shipwreck Without a Thrill.......................51
The Wreck of the Chaparra...........................55
Lost in the Fog..57
Lost and Presumed Drowned......................... 60
A War of Words.......................................62
The Nazis Sink the Gulftrade.........................68
Nazis "Invade" Long Beach Island...................70
Collision At Sea.......................................73
The Ghostly Mast..................................... 76
The Stolt Dagali: Sheared in Two.................... 79
"Never a Night So Long"..............................82
The Christmas Storm of '09...........................87
The Sea Raiders...................................... 88
Steering to Death.....................................89
Wrecks By Design.....................................91

If by your art, my dearest father,
you have
Put the wild waters in this roar,
allay them.
The sky, it seems would pour down
stinking pitch.
But that the sea, mounting to the
welkin's cheek,
Dashes the fire out. O, I have suffer'd
With those that I saw suffer! A
brave vessel,
Dash'd all to pieces. O, the cry did
knock
Against my very heart! Poor souls,
they perish'd!
Had I been any god of power,
I would
Have sunk the sea within the earth,
or ere
It should the good ship so have
swallo'd and
The fraughting souls within her.

William Shakespeare
"The Tempest"
ca. 1610 A.D.

FOREWORD
to the 1984 Edition

Even before New Jersey coastal travel and shipping became logistically important, the treacherous Barnegat Shoals have held the reputation of being one of the most dangerous navigational hazards along our eastern coast.

Literally hundreds of ships have succumbed to the powers of the sea, and within view of the Barnegat Lighthouse beam.

If it wouldn't be for the disguising and deteriorating effects of the shifting sand, waves, salt, teredo worms and storm winds, the Barnegat Shoals and surrounding area would be an underwater junkyard for boats, ships and cargo.

But nature rebels to the intrusion of wrecked hulks littering the ocean floor and beach, and she has a way of returning her realm to a natural, unmolested state. In a matter of a few years a sunken, beached and abandoned ship can be completely covered by sand; or a storm will break it into small pieces. Or, if it is made of wood, the destructive teredo worms will devour it in a few decades.

It has been said, and this is probably an understatement, there has been an average of a shipwreck every quarter-mile along the coastal area of the infamous Barnegat Inlet. Therefore, even though the ship disaster stories within these pages are factual accounts, they represent only a small percentage of the actual shipwreck events that have emanated from this area.

SHIPWRECKS NEAR BARNEGAT INLET

Many have fished, scuba dived, motored and sailed over these wrecks. Many divers have searched the crevices, nooks and crannies of these wrecks for lobsters or "bugs," as divers call them, and some have been lucky enough to catch one of fifteen or more pounds.

Others have at least come up with a "goodie bag" loaded with large, sweet-tasting mussels. The fishing over these wrecks has usually proven to be outstanding, with a shipwreck being an underwater oasis for many species of fish.

Those who play on and over these shipwrecks and portions thereof don't know the events that placed each hull at its resting place. Bathers may be walking, surfing and swimming over the remains of an old sailing ship that was driven ashore many years ago, and has by now broken apart and sunk many feet under the sand.

So, here's a collection of true stories of some of the more widely-known shipwrecks near Barnegat Inlet. All stories are documented through research in the National Archives in Washington D.C., United States Coast Guard records, contemporary newspaper accounts, and even some word-of-mouth reports as to the events of each disaster in this book.

David J. Seibold
Barnegat Light, N.J.
June, 1984

INTRODUCTION
to the 1984 Edition

What mortal is not fascinated by the sea? Man is of the sea, and forever shall man feel a strong kinship with the sea. He has welcomed its cooling waves. He has harvested its bounty. He has taken upon it in vessels both small and mighty.

Fully aware that the power, the torment and the rage of the oceans is far greater than he can ever hope to conquer, he has sought to conquer it still, for eons.

Along the New Jersey coastline between the haggard honkytonks and shameless shipyards there lies an island. It is a magical place, ever formed and re-formed by the ocean's whim. The long sandy beaches of this island's eastern strand gave it the name we use today: Long Beach Island.

Oh, what stories the beaches, bogs and hillocks could tell! But even these features, while seemingly permanent in relation to the life of a man, are but moments within the life of the sea and the lands which attempt to confine it.

We cannot own a piece of the sea. We stand in awe from a rockbound coast and revel in its ceaseless assault. We are, perhaps, calmed by the erratic rhythm. We wander through piers and harbors and our imaginations are tantalized by the romance of ships and the sea.

Indeed, what man is not fascinated by all of this?

Long Beach Island is the embodiment of everything that is of this fascination—this infatuation. Commercial fishing craft vie for their pieces of the sea with the pleasure boats that also call this water their own.

SHIPWRECKS NEAR BARNEGAT INLET

There are the people who call this island home. There are the people who use it as a release valve for the landlocked realities.

The Indians of this land knew the island well. They, too, reaped its bounty, without raping its beauty. White men, settlers from far-of lands, certainly did not force this narrow barrier island into submission. Theirs was to be a romantic encounter only.

Certainly in many ways it still is, but the deflowering of the virgin littoral has taken place, despite the angry and often savage protestations of nature.

What white man first set eyes on this land from a tempest-tossed wooden shell? Was it the seemingly ubiquitous Leif Ericson, who some say passed by some fifteen years short of Christianity's first one-thousand years? Was it some other anonymous adventurer whose deeds have been lost in time?

Or was it Captain Cornelius Mey, who in 1614 adapted the Dutch word for "inlet breakers" and named the shoreline "Barendegat"?

From Barendegat came Barnegat, and for more than a century, the island was called "Old Barnegat Beach." As the sailors came to know the island's bays, inlets and beaches, they charted and plotted and found courses between the barriers.

Their determination to tame the brutal inlet at the island's northern tip resulted in "Old Barney," the landmark lighthouse that still today pokes its peak through the fog, high over land and sea.

Off the coast of Long Beach Island, hundreds—nay, thousands—of men and women have been sent to their deaths by the pounding waves and breakers. The loss of 38 souls aboard the packet ship **John Minturn** as it ran aground near the island led to the formation of a formal Life Saving Service after 1846.

Ah, yes, if only the sands could speak to us!

SHIPWRECKS NEAR BARNEGAT INLET

They might tell of the history and mystery of Long Beach Island. It was near the island's southern shore where the redoubtable "Old Ironsides" sailed into a formation of five Redcoat men-of-war on a hot July day in 1776.

Pitifully overmatched, the **USS Constitution** held her ground, er, her water, and fought valiantly before slipping away in a storm to the open seas and safety.

The sands would tell of pirates.

They would tell the story of American privateer Andrew Steel, who discovered a derelict British cutter filled with valuable cargo floating aimlessly about a mile south of Barnegat Inlet. The crew of his ship, the **Alligator**, was joined by other ne'er-do-wells from Barnegat and Waretown and began to transfer the cargo from the abandoned British freighter to the **Alligator**.

The cargo was to cumbersome for one day's work, so the self-appointed salvagers rowed to the beach for a night's rest.

Hearing of the situation, Captain John Bacon assembled his pirate crew at his base at Island Beach, on the north side of Barnegat Inlet.

In the middle of the night, as the salvagers lay sleeping on the beach, the cutthroats slipped silently to Long Beach Island, surprised the slumbering privateers, and murdered all but five of the 26 in the camp.

Perhaps the ghosts of these men walk the northern beach of Long Beach Island today.

Perhaps the shadows on the sea and the haunting groans and whispers one hears where the sea meets the shore are the groans and whispers of those who have become one with the sea; those who have been lost forever beneath the waves.

What you are about to read is not intended to be an historical document. All is accurate, all is well-researched and documented. But it is important to remember that this book is merely a collection of stories from the long, often

5

glorious and often gloomy history of the shores of Long Beach Island.

Let the exact positions, LORAN readings and such to the serious diver and fisherman. Much of this has been researched, but in the interest of popular acceptance, it has been omitted.

Let the minute details of each wreck to the maritime historian. They would doubtlessly compile a more text-like (and tedious) volume.

Let your imagination run rampant for a few hours.

As you read these stories of drama off Long Beach Island, remember...dream...ponder...enjoy.

Charles J. Adams III
Barnegat Light, N.J.
June, 1984

INTRODUCTION TO THE REVISED, UPDATED EDITION

by Charles J. Adams III, 1995

Eleven years have passed since the publication of the first edition of *Shipwrecks Near Barnegat Inlet.*

The book marked the first time Dave Seibold and I combined to research, write, organize and publish a book.

Our choice then of computer typesetting was hasty and primitive. Our choice of printer, paper, binding, etc., was predicated on price and based on the queasiness of our freshman publishing experience.

Would anyone buy the book? Would we recuperate even enough money to meet even our minimal expenses? Would we end up papering our walls with pages from *Shipwrecks Near Barnegat Inlet* and never again do something as silly as publish our own book?

More than a dozen books and more than a decade later, our questions have been answered. We have found a certain niche in our reasonably-priced books on ghosts, legends, shipwrecks and train accidents, and we have learned much about the publishing game over the years.

As we examined the book which started it all, we found a product in need of attention and a topic in need of updating and expanding.

The entire text of the 1984 edition of *Shipwrecks* is included in this edition, but in a more appealing typeface and layout.

More photographs and shipwreck stories have been added, and we hope the result will prove interesting.

THE DEATH
OF A "DOUBLE-ENDER"

During the Civil War, the United States found a need for swift, solid, versatile crafts that would be able to navigate in shallow waters to prowl and protect coastal inlets, bays and rivers.

Even the minimal draft of one of these, the **South Carolina**, failed to stave off the destruction dealt by the Barnegat Shoals.

The **South Carolina** was one of a half-dozen so-called "double-enders" built in Boston by Harris, Loring and Company for service in the war.

By "double-ender," it is meant that the vessels were equipped with steering apparati both fore and aft. This particular fast, iron sidewheel steamer was christened as the **Winnipeg**, but following her wartime service she was redubbed the **South Carolina** when sold to civilian owners.

In about 1870, the ship was rebuilt and outfitted for merchant trade by her new owner, W.B. Clyde of Philadelphia.

The double-ender was also a double-decker, well suited for transport of drygoods and cotton, which she was carrying the day she went down at Barnegat.

The sun was just rising the morning of December 22, 1874, and Captain J.T. Beckett and his crew of 24 were probably thinking of the Christmas on shore they were to have in a couple days when they arrive in New York after their cruise up the coast from Charleston.

8

SHIPWRECKS NEAR BARNEGAT INLET

The cruise ended abruptly when the wicked winds of December sent the 255-foot, 1,609-ton ship crashing into the shoals.

Immediately, Captain Beckett ordered the cargo jettisoned, to lighten the ship and hopefully refloat her. This would not happen. By 9:40 a.m., Life-Saving boats arrived from Forked River and Barnegat City to rescue the crew members. All were taken to safety at J.W. Kinsey's Boarding House in Barnegat City.

For hours, the cargo was tossed overboard, but to no avail. The ship was hopelessly mired on the shoals and the damage was done.

The Coast Wrecking Company was summoned to the scene, and worked throughout the day to free the ship from the grip of Barnegat Shoals. Try as they may have, the relentless, magnetic shoals had claimed another victim.

¤

SHREDS OF EVIDENCE

Because of the nature of their construction, and of the powerful undertow and currents of the Barnegat Shoals and its approaches, many ship wrecked here in the mid-to-late 19th century are no longer in any way intact on the ocean floor.

Time, tides and tempests have broken them into shards of evidence, barely discernible even by the most sophisticated underwater sounding gear.

Because of the bits and pieces left, often buried under bottom sand, only the most seasoned seaman can determine a "wreck" even when it is charted and marked.

Two vessels that have been pounded into pieces, and of which little evidence remains are the **Mediator** and the **Simila**. Both fell victims of the turbulent seas around Barnegat Inlet and both have become somewhat vacuous monuments in the graveyard of ships off Long Beach Island.

The **Mediator** was shipping drygoods and groceries from Port Royal to New York under the Lorillard flag. One of two Lorillard steamers operated by the Port Royal and Fernandina Steamship Company, the 320-foot, double-decked, oak-hulled ship was barely two years old when she went down (or in her case, "up").

The tide was in at the northernmost point of Barnegat Shoals at 6:30 in the morning, January 22, 1875. The choppy sea was speckled with ice floes, and the Mediator had weathered a long, frigid, foggy night.

Without warning, the ship's screws began to churn up sand. The ship was going to run aground. The chief officer

10

and his 19-man crew watched helplessly as the sea had its way. The steamer ground to a halt in about ten feet of water, within easy sight of land.

The men of the **Mediator** were saved, and a wrecking company removed the ship's cargo, except for some hay. But the **Mediator** was doomed. In short order, the seas began to crush the bulkheads and weaken the vessel's hull. The **Mediator** slipped beneath the waves and died an agonizing death.

Two Januaries later, the 179-foot, 1,110-ton **Simila**, built in Portsmouth, New Hampshire in 1863, fell prey to a violent gale from the east, and was tossed on the shore about six miles below Barnegat Inlet.

The wooden-hulled sailing ship carried a crew of twenty, and was in ballast on her voyage from Marseilles to America. There was no cargo aboard.

The storm showed no mercy on the **Simila**. Life-Saving crews from Harvey Cedars and Ship Bottom managed to save all crew members, but the ship broke up quickly in the surging surf.

These are but two of the shipwrecks along Long Beach island that were not "front page news." There will be no great works of art depicting these wrecks. There was not enough drama to warrant movie or a book.

There are no poems to be written, or memorials to the memory of the **Simila** or **Mediator** to be erected.

But, the agony aboard both vessels on those days so very long ago can still be felt by anyone who has experienced the power of the sea.

¤

DOWN WITH HIS SHIP

The years were unkind to the brig **Frank Clark**.

Barely eleven years at sea, the ship was showing the scars of the tough North Atlantic coastal trade. Built in Damariscotta, Maine, in 1867, the **Frank Clark** was to meet her destruction in a collision with a schooner in the darkness of Friday Night, February 21, 1876, just beyond the outer shoals of Barnegat.

Seas were running high that evening, and the **Frank Clark** was bound on a northeasterly course, heading for New York from St. Thomas.

Approaching from the opposite direction was the schooner **Adelaide J. Alcott**, maintaining a course for Virginia. The **Alcott** was running light, with no cargo aboard.

A lookout aboard the **Alcott** reported seeing the **Frank Clark** in the distance. All was well, he and the helmsman agreed, for the running lights indicated a smooth passage, port to port. The tricky sea would have to be reckoned with, but there appeared to be no danger.

Suddenly, the **Clark** changed course. She steered toward the land, and within minutes the two vessels were but a hundred yards apart with the **Alcott** bearing down on the **Clark**.

Frantically, the **Alcott's** wheel spun at the command of its captain.

The ship plunged into the waves, its helmsman's muscles desperately straining to bring her about an avoid the inevitable.

12

SHIPWRECKS NEAR BARNEGAT INLET

With a thundering crash, the **Alcott's** bow thrust into the **Clark**, striking the hapless brig a bit aft of the forward rigging.

It was all over for the **Frank Clark**. In an instant, the salt water began filling her compartments. Within twenty minutes, she was down six fathoms. The ship's foremast and stern protruded above the surface, mute reminders of the collision and eerie grave markers for the three who perished.

Those three were the **Frank Clark's** captain, Samuel Morton, his wife and the ship's first mate. All other in the crew swam through the icy water to safety aboard the ship that had struck the **Clark**.

These seven surviving crew men managed to rescue two youngsters, the adopted children of Capt. and Mrs. Morton. But, they could not save their parents. The couple, and the mate, were caught below decks when the **Alcott** ripped into the **Clark**. They never knew what hit them.

The **Alcott** remained at the scene throughout the night, searching the surface for any traces of the missing. The search was called off shortly after daybreak.

Captain Morton, more than likely unaware, but in the truest tradition of his kind, had gone down with his ship.

¤

13

THE PIE-EYED PILOT AND THE WRECK OF THE MAGNUS

The following tale includes little in the way of tragedy or high drama on the high seas. The vessel involved was a nondescript brig carrying a relatively bland cargo and all hands as well as the ship itself were saved.

But if there can be some "comic relief" in an otherwise dour collection of nautical nightmares, this story will stand as that.

The **Magnus** was bound from Guttenburgh, Sweden, to New York–after securing her cargo of 3,800 bags of sugar in the tropics. The Swedish-registry ship was under the command of a Captain Edstrom, a respected master who served his ship and his employer well.

The **Magnus'** voyage up the coast of New Jersey was unremarkable, and on April 18, 1877, she coasted to Absecon where a veteran pilot was put aboard to guide the brig up the tricky coastline to New York.

This pilot's name has faded into oblivion, and but for this account, his deeds may also have been forgotten. But whomever he may have been, his actions in the wee, small hours of April 19, 1877 are preserved here forever.

The captain and crew of the **Magnus** probably noticed something peculiar about this crusty Jersey Coast helmsman when he boarded their ship. No doubt, their suspicions were confirmed at 3 a.m. as the ship drifted dangerously close to the shore of northern Long Beach Island.

14

SHIPWRECKS NEAR BARNEGAT INLET

As confusion reigned aboard the **Magnus**, the ship fought to remain seabound. The finger of fate (and the hand of the pilot) had different ideas. The crew could smell the land. The surf pounded against the sides of the brig and heaved it westward.

A thud...a scraping sound...the ship was aground!

There she lay. About five miles south of Barnegat Inlet, near what was then Joseph Ridgeway's Hotel, the **Magnus** was propped up, looking like a forlorn, beached, wooden whale.

Life-Saving crews from Barnegat City and Loveladies sped to the scene. The ship was intact and basically undamaged. The coast wrecking steamer **Relief** came later to pump out the brig and unload her cargo. The men escaped injuries and the **Magnus** was pulled from the shoals and refloated.

Oh yes, what of the pilot? What was so "peculiar" about him? What drove him to run the **Magnus** aground when he was hired to guide her safely through the last hundred miles of her voyage?

He was drunk.

Dead drunk.

Blitzed to the gills!

Yes, even then, and even in the sea lanes off Long Beach Island, drunken "driving" was taking its toll!

✡

A SHOCKING ARRIVAL

For sixty-three German immigrants, intent on making a new life in the rolling hills of Texas, landfall in America was to be a shocking experience and, quite literally, a "fall" onto the land!

The Deutschlanders were aboard the red-hulled, schooner-rigged steamer **Guadalupe**, along with four cabin passengers and the crew.

The 2,839-ton vessel was built just three years before its demise. The iron ship rolled into the Delaware River from the John Roach Shipyard in Chester in 1881. She was pressed into service by her owners, the W.H. Mallory Company, and on November 19, 1884 she was carrying a load of railroad iron, farm machinery and miscellaneous cargo.

There was little reason to suspect anything untoward was to take place that night. A stiff breeze wafted across her decks, but the seas were generally calm.

At about 8 p.m., Captain Nickerson of the **Guadalupe** complained of feeling ill and retired to his cabin. The ship was turned over to the next in command. The mate was new and unfamiliar with the idiosyncrasies of the steamer and likely just as unaware of the dangers lurking around Barnegat Shoals.

All was quiet aboard the ship as it continued along the coastline. For all intents and purposes, it was a routine passage.

16

SHIPWRECKS NEAR BARNEGAT INLET

Suddenly, without any warning, the ship ground to a halt. Well within sight of Island Beach, the **Guadalupe** rested helplessly on the sandy shoals. An eerie mixture of English and German erupted as crew and passengers were shaken from their peaceful late-evening repose. Dozens of people rushed to the deck to see what had happened.

Crew members made a quick but thorough assessment of damages. Thankfully, they found no major problems. The passengers' fears were allayed and the bilingual cacophony subsided.

Now and then a wave would break over the bow of the ship as it lay dead in the water. The passengers were told to return to their berths and the crew was assembled to await orders from their under-the-weather captain, whose much-needed rest was so abruptly disturbed.

Personnel in the Life-Saving Stations at Forked River and Barnegat City noticed the lights of the **Guadalupe**, seemingly stationary in the area of the dangerous shoals, just a couple miles from the beach.

They maintained a watch on the vessel, but saw not rockets or flares, and cautiously believed the ship was not in distress.

Through the night, shipboard investigators noticed their seafaring steed was taking on some water, but the damage was not believed to be serious. Despite the obvious predicament they found themselves in, all aboard the **Guadalupe** had a relatively restful night.

When the sun lit the eastern sky, however, it was obvious to those on the ship and those on shore that the Barnegat Shoals were not about to release their captive.

The weather had turned a bit more foul, and Captain Reuben Tilton of the Forked River Station summoned help. Lifeboats from the Forked River, Barnegat City, Loveladies and Cedar Creek stations made their way to the stricken ship, and the sight of this massive rescue effort finally convinced the folks aboard the **Guadalupe** that the ship had to be

17

abandoned.

There was but one ladder over the sides of the steamer, so one-by-one, the passengers were helped onto the smallboats. All were saved, taken to shore safely and placed on a New Jersey Southern railroad car for passage to New York City.

There still remained the question of the fate of the ship itself. The Merritt Coast Wrecking Company was called in to salvage what could be salvaged. Most of the heavy equipment and other bulk cargo was retrieved. It was thought that the lighter ship could now be easily towed from the shoal.

A determined salvage crew worked to save the **Guadalupe**, but the forces of the sea eventually won out. The ship broke apart at midships and sank as a total loss.

Following the incident, the daring men of the Life-Saving Stations were commended by the **Guadalupe**'s captain, crew, and passengers, as well as by local residents and the superintendent of the fourth Life-Saving District. Their bravery and unflappable professionalism was praised, and once again the service provided by these dedicated souls was proven to be worthwhile and vital.

✡

LIFE-SAVERS TO THE RESCUE!

The heroics of the Life-Saving Stations that dotted the New Jersey coastline long ago are detailed throughout this volume. This chapter, however, is a brief review of several wrecks in and around Barnegat Inlet that resulted in great loss in property and cargo, but because of the Life-Savers, no loss of life.

The bark **Aberdeen** was built during the Civil War and was still plying the Eastern Seaboard on January 6, 1885. The ship would see no service beyond that date, though, as she was victimized by the heavy fog that all-too-often lingers offshore.

Amazingly, the **Aberdeen** was to join another ship of the same name that sank thirty years before in the same area. Records of that earlier loss are virtually impossible to retrieve.

Cotton and hemp stuffed the holds of the **Aberdeen** as

19

she made her voyage from Mobile, Alabama, to Boston. Captain Robert P. Conk was the master, and even the most seasoned veteran of coastal sailing—as he was—could easily fall prey to the fogs of Barnegat.

Feeling her way through the muck, the **Aberdeen** coasted too far inland and became embedded in the sands near the shore. She was just opposite the Harvey Cedars Life-Saving Station when, at 6:30 a.m., she ran aground.

Within minutes, the men of the Harvey Cedars Station rowed out to assist in the rescue. But despite the proximity of the wreck to the rescuers, the task was not carried out without a hitch.

That hitch was the tide. There was some trouble encountered when the Life-Savers arrived on board the **Aberdeen**.

Errors were made when lines were attached, and adjustments had to be made to ensure a safe rescue. By the time those adjustments were completed, however, the tide had risen to a point where the seas were too turbulent for such assurance. The Life-Savers elected to stay aboard the **Aberdeen** until the tide receded and the sea calmed.

By that time, Captain Grimm and the crew of the Loveladies Life-Saving Station arrived to help. Within about forty minutes, the crew of the **Aberdeen** was landed ashore safely.

Mired in some eight feet of sand, the **Aberdeen** was obviously a total loss. There was no insurance on the vessel itself, but the carrier covering the cargo immediately recruited a crew to salvage as much of the cargo as possible.

•

The seas off Long Beach Island were truly "sweetened" on May 23, 1901 when the Italian bark **Bianca Aspasia** struck a sand bar about a mile and a half north of Ship Bottom.

Once again, the Life-Savers came to the rescue, saving all fifteen crew men aboard the 466-ton ship bound from

20

SHIPWRECKS NEAR BARNEGAT INLET

Santo Domingo to New York.

Immobile just off the beach, those on the **Bianca Aspasia** watched as the rescuers shot the first line toward their vessel. It was far off its mark. A second line unfurled over the ship, but the crew could not rig the tackle.

Seeing that this rescue method was futile, a boat was launched from the Ship Bottom station and after several trips, the crew and its baggage was safely hustled ashore.

The Merritt Wrecking Company was summoned to pry the ship from the bar, but to no avail. After several days, this salvage attempt was abandoned and the ship was left to the hands of nature.

Oh, yes, the cargo of the **Bianca Aspasia**?

It was sugar. Tons of sugar. And, as the salt water seeped into the hold of the bark, a most unusual concoction was mixed!

¤

A similar anomaly took place in the early morning hours of August 12, 1928, when a load of fish was returned to the sea when the fishing smack **Sara H. Blaisdel** was thrown ashore on Island Beach just south of Seaside Heights.

Berthed at Sheepshead Bay, New York, the 47-foot trawler was fishing off Manasquan when it developed engine trouble. It was about 2 a.m. when Captain Van derklooster and his three-man crew began to drift south. By seven that morning, the boat was sighted by Captain Louis Mitchell of the Island Beach Coast Guard Station, foundering in heavy seas.

Those seas were so heavy for the comparatively small boat that a giant wave literally picked it up and tossed it like a toy onto a sand bar.

Three crew men were washed overboard, but managed to struggle back to the deck. Another wave crashed into the **Blaisdel** and carried her back from the shore. In an instant, yet another heavy roll lifted the ship toward the beach and succeeding waves battered her to bits.

21

SHIPWRECKS NEAR BARNEGAT INLET

Coast Guard crew men fought the oncoming surges and managed to rescue the four crew men. One of them had suffered a broken leg.

The ship and her catch were lost, with damages estimated at $15,000.

¤

Barnegat Life-Saving Station No. 17 was typical of the many structures which once lined the New Jersey shore. From these quarters, surfmen awaited the call of distress from a troubled vessel. Several of the ancient structures have survived the decades and are utilized for residential or commercial use.

HEROICS, SURVIVAL AND DEATH

The following story contains elements of the very best and the very worst of what can happen in the course and aftermath of a shipwreck.

The darkness and bone-cracking cold of the dead of winter on the seas off Long Beach Island must be experienced to be fully understood. Move back a century, before modern navigational equipment and creature-comforting conveniences aboard ship, and the scenario is even more frightening.

It was February 10, 1886, 1:30 in the morning. The bark **Kraljevica** was sailing close–too close–to the Jersey coast when the south shoals of Barnegat punched through her hull, adding her cargo of salt to the already briny depths.

The weather had made navigation along the coast very dangerous. Captain Sverjuga and his crew of thirteen from Fiume, Austria, were bound from Marseilles to New York with their shipment, but only six of the Austrians were ever to see another sunrise.

The **Kraljevica** struck the shoals with no warning. The crew scrambled for the longboat, after sending a rocket flare skyward to alert anyone on shore of their plight.

The surf crashed incessantly into the longboat, eventually capsizing it and sending eight of the men to their deaths. The other six grabbed the sides of the boat and clung together. Miraculously, the survivors struggled the half-mile to the beach and limped ashore to find any kind of shelter that

23

would ease their pain inflicted by the ordeal in the 39-degree water.

What they found was a box built for duck hunters. They found food and fuel and somehow weathered the night. The weather had turned even more foul and a blizzard-like storm pelted the beach.

While the men of the **Kraljevica** huddled together in hopes of being discovered and taken to safety, another drama was being played out nearby.

The flare sent up by the crew men on the doomed bark did not go unnoticed. Captain Ridgeway of the Barnegat City coast watch station saw the rocket pierce the night sky and ordered the station's boat launched.

It is nearly impossible to believed what happened next, but in these more "enlightened" days, it is almost impossible to imagine the resolve and dedication of the men of the rescue details of the New Jersey coastline a hundred years ago.

The Life-Savers fought against the searing gale winds and rabid surf to reach the distressed bark. Rowing, straining, every ounce of courage and strength being put to the ultimate test, the crew battled its way for two grueling hours and came within fifty yards of the stricken vessel only to have their hopes crushed. They had no idea that the crew had abandoned ship.

The crestfallen rescue-boat crew had little time to linger in their frustration. The storm had turned even nastier, but at least the northeastern wind would make their return trip a bit easier–they thought.

Anxious to return to safety, the men brought their boat around and made for the shore. But about 400 yards from that sandy haven, a massive swell overturned the Life-Saving boat, drowning three of the men.

The others managed to make it home, their comrades the victims of the same sea they had hoped to conquer by their chosen endeavor.

The survivors of the **Kraljevica** who had spent their

night in the duck blind were saved. Their ship was torn to pieces by the nor'easter, and the people of Barnegat City mourned their fallen heroes.

So, too, did the people of Austria.

The Austrian government was so impressed by the unselfish deeds of the Life-Saving crew that they established a fund for the families of the surfmen who gave their lives in an attempt to save the crew of the **Kraljevica**.

The three dead men were buried in Barnegat, and through an act of the United States Congress, a majestic marble monument was erected over each grave.

◻

THE "WENDT" WASHES ASHORE

Few seaside spectacles compare to the sight of a fully-rigged sailing vessel washed up on the beach. It is a sight that belongs to past generations, and would be a rare occurrence today or in the future.

Such a prospect is all the more fascinating when there is no loss of life, as was the case in the grounding of the 2,369-ton **J.W. Wendt**.

It was March 21, 1889. The **Wendt** was at sea one month to the day, having shoved off from Bremen, Germany, bound for New York with her holds full of iron.

For several days, the ship's captain, a man named Lass, was confused as to the position of the vessel.

The ship drifted far off course, to the point where neither captain nor navigator could determine exactly where they were. They were shaken into the realization that they were so far to leeward when the tell-tale scraping of the ship's keel warned them they were about to run aground.

Run aground the big ship did, some three miles north of Barnegat Inlet. As the wood-hulled ship shivered to a halt, the captain shouted orders to "hard up," but it was too late.

Ships are built to withstand the undulating motion of the sea, and can generally take anything the waves can throw at them. The immovable earth, however, is something few ships are designed to encounter.

The **Wendt** crashed into the beach and with the abrupt impact, the massive timber masts snapped as if they were

26

toothpicks. As the masts toppled and crashed to the deck, they tore gaping holes in the vessel.

The sea water rushed into every crack and crevice of the crumbling hull.

Clinging to what was left of the ship, the crew members hung on in the icy, storm-tossed sea until life-saving crews arrived to rescue all thirty men.

The **Wendt**, which was built in 1853 and christened the **Morning Light** for service under the British flag, had been the pride of the German fleet. For years after she was sold to Siedenburg, Wendt & Co. of Bremen, she served her masters. She was one of the largest ships flying the German flag at the time.

That day on Long Beach Island, the ship was a total loss, at least to her owners. Damages were estimated at $32,000, and the wreck was a pitiable sight as it rested on the beach. As a child's castaway boat in a sandbox, it remained until local fishermen and others stripped its beamed bones clean of what, to them, was valuable lumber.

INFERNO AT SEA

Many years before the eastern horizon beyond Long Beach Island was set aglow by burning merchant ship gutted by Nazi torpedoes, there was another eerie sight to behold.

On occasion, the townsfolk of the villages on shore could glimpse what a *New Jersey Courier* writer once called a "magnificent but awe-inspiring spectacle." It was the view across miles of ocean to a distant ship engulfed in flames.

Such an emblazonry would glow as a false sunrise. Those on shore would watch with helpless agony as the drama would play out.

The 1,279-ton steamer **Delaware** died in one such fiery incident on July 9, 1898.

The 251-foot vessel was built to Bireby, Hillman and Streaker in Philadelphia in 1880. Originally a freighter, she served for more than a dozen years in that capacity until her owner, the Clyde Line Company, chartered her to the United States government for use as a transport. The ship, built of yellow pine and oak with iron and copper fittings, was valued at $125,000.

Captain A.D. Ingram had worked for the Clyde Line for 21 years. When he received his captain's license, he was the youngest man ever to do so. He had been master of the **Delaware** for twelve years, and was to lead the ship into her new role as an Army transport. The Wilmington, North Carolina, native never dreamed the **Delaware's** "maiden

28

voyage" as a transport would be her last.

The **Delaware** was heavily laden with miscellaneous drygoods for the U.S. Army. She left Pier 29 on New York's East River at 3:30 p.m., July 9, also carrying her crew of 38 plus a passenger contingent of 24 men, eight women and three children.

Bound for Charleston, South Carolina and then to Jacksonville, Florida, the **Delaware** cruised out of New York harbor and set a course just off the Jersey coast.

The wreck of the **Delaware** was not the result of the dangerous shoals or a collision in soupy fog. Somehow, and there is little historical reference as to how or why, a fire broke out in the aft hold at about 9:30 p.m., July 9.

The blaze was already well underway when discovered, but the captain and others tried to extinguish it. There was no use. Interested in the safety of many people aboard, Captain Ingram ordered the launching of four lifeboats. The tradition of "women and children first" was adhered to, with First Officer McBeth guiding these folks in the first boat away. The second boat was reserved for the male passengers, in command of Seaman Porter.

Aboard the **Delaware**, which was rapidly being ravaged by the flames, Captain Ingram ignited two Coston lights to alert any ships and/or the shorebound life-savers. The **Delaware** was in trouble about five miles off shore, some five miles north of Barnegat Light. Upon first notice of the signal lights, the men of Life-Saving Station 15 at Cedar Creek took to their boat.

At the same time, a pair ships began to converge on the site of the emergency. As the fire consumed the wooden ship and flames shot into the night sky, the sloop **S.P. Miller** sped to render assistance. She remained there to take some of the passengers from the lifeboats. The tug **Ocean King** was also in the vicinity. She anchored the two coal barges she was towing and took the remaining passengers aboard.

The two remaining lifeboats were not large enough to

accommodate the entire crew. One of the boats, in command of the second mate, nearly became the funeral pyre for those who boarded it. When the boat was filled with crew men, it was discovered that the drain plug was missing. The boat quickly filled with water as the men tried to plug the drain hole.

Frantically, they fought the rush of the water. Several men leaped overboard while others stuffed the hole with handkerchiefs and proceeded to bail out the water. While all this was going on, the **Delaware** was turning into a raging inferno. Those on that troubled boat suffered burn blisters on their faces and hands as the result of their struggle alongside the doomed ship.

The captain and several other men were in another fix. These senior officers elected to allow the crew members to fill all available space on the lifeboats. The crafty mariners rigged a makeshift raft using hatch combings and gratings and made their escape.

None of the those who abandoned the **Delaware** had to wait long for their rescue. Captain Ingram expressed surprise at the short time it took for the life-savers from Cedar Creek to make it to the scene.

The captain and officers were picked up by the life-saving crew, and landed at the Cedar Creek Station before being transferred to Barnegat Pier and then by rail to New York.

Throughout the trying minutes it took to abandon the ship, there were many reports of personal heroism. One engine room attendant, staying at his post until it was obviously no use, was cut off from the captain and officers who were the last to leave. This crewman, whose name has been lost in history, was forced to jump overboard. He was picked up by one of the other lifeboats and suffered second-degree burns of his neck, arms and back.

Another man, Chief Engineer Platt, feared the ship's boilers would blow and cause great loss of life. He scrambled below, fighting the flames, and turned off the steam.

The **Delaware** remained afloat throughout the night of July 9 and well into the next day. A helpless derelict, she burned herself out and drifted slowly toward the beach. The ship and cargo were lost, and debris washed up on shore from Bay Head to Barnegat Light. All that was left were charred timbers. What substantial portions were left were sold for scrap.

For weeks, beachcombers scoured the sand, seeking souvenirs from the wreck of the **Delaware**. Everything from life jackets, burnt wood and cork was collected.

Some call the remains of the **Delaware** "The Money Wreck" because its close proximity to shore enables charter captains to transport adventurous divers to the site even on "down days" of bad weather.

Even today, the sea occasionally gives up the remains of the incinerated hulk. Who knows? That aged, ashen artifact found on the sand on and around Island Beach State Park, just may be a relic from the wreck of the **Delaware** so very long ago!

¤

THE SHIP OF DEATH

It could be said that the schooner **Wilson and Hunting** was truly a "death ship."

If nothing else, it proved to be the vehicle of death of two brothers from a proud seagoing family.

For generations, the Waltons had gone to sea. In 1904, three men representing two generations of Waltons were at the helms of East Coast merchant vessels.

Captain Robert I. Walton Sr. was master of the **Henry P. Haven** out of Norfolk, Virginia. His sons, Robert Jr. and Clarence, were waiting in the maritime wings to continue the family tradition.

Clarence Walton had already achieved the ultimate as master of the **Wilson and Hunting**. She was a 418-ton, 145-foot ship built in 1883 at Alexandria, Virginia.

It was aboard that ship that Clarence contracted typhoid fever. During a layover in the port of Philadelphia, the devils of the disease ravaged his body and soul. In a helpless state of delirium, Clarence Walton took a gun to his head and pulled the trigger. His suicide on February 1, 1904, nearly devastated the family.

As if by divine right, though, brother Robert I. Walton Jr. came to take command of the **Wilson and Hunting**. No doubt the memory of his brother's misfortune lived with him aboard the vessel, but he knew what had to be done.

Robert Walton was no stranger to the sea, and fewer

than six months before his brother's suicide, he too had a brush with death.

He was master of the three-masted schooner **De Mory-Gray** when, on September 15, 1903, a terrible hurricane attacked the ship about ten miles northeast of Winter Quarter Shoals. For hours, the winds and waves tested the crew and ship. Aboard was Robert's wife, Etta, who sailed with her husband on occasion. As the hurricane blasted the ship, Walton sought to protect his wife. He lashed her to the mizzen crosstrees, where she would stand a fair chance of survival, should the ship go down.

His worst fears were not realized, however. The ship weathered the storm, and after an hour the harried woman was released from her perilous perch.

In the course of their lives together at sea, this was to become a mere footnote. Six years later, they were to die together at the hands of the sea.

One could call the deaths of Robert and Emma Walton on November 9, 1904 a "freak accident." Others could (and did) term it a result of the violation of the oceanic "rules of the road" by a United States government refrigerator ship.

The steward of the **Wilson and Hunting** was one of the survivors of the collision between that schooner and the steamer, **Culgoa**. He told his story the day after the tragedy.

"I was stuck in the galley when the schooner was struck. We were holding our course on a port tack off shore. Shortly before I went below, I saw the lamp on top of the cabin burning brightly. The steamer cam on us apparently at full speed, and struck us to starboard, aft of the forward rigging. When I reached the deck I climbed up the rigging and got aboard the **Culgoa**, the bow of which was wedged well into our schooner.

"Soon after I got aboard the mate followed my plan of escape, but when he reached the rigging, the steamer reversed her engines and the boats swayed apart. The mate plunged into the sea and the **Culgoa** lowered a boat to get him. The

33

schooner was laden with piling, stored on the deck eight feet high. The captain and his wife were on deck, and could have been rescued had not the **Culgoa** backed away.

"The instant the boats separated, the schooner filled, her deck load shifted and she listed to starboard and sank, taking the captain and his wife with her."

Another survivor of the wreck said the lookout on the schooner had noticed the lights of the approaching steamer, and reckoned that a clear passage would be made. The schooner continued on its port tack, and according to the law of the sea, had the right of way.

Suddenly, the lookout noticed that the steamer was not yielding to the sailing ship. The captain was alerted, and within seconds, both he and Mrs. Walton rushed to the deck. In a glance, Captain Walton ordered a distress flare displayed, fully aware that collision was imminent.

The steamer struck, lifting the side of the schooner high out of the water. The heavy timber, precariously placed on deck, crashed down. The second witness to the incident maintained that the captain, his wife and two other crew men were crushed by the timber before they reached the water.

The **Wilson and Hunting** was a total loss. Her cargo spilled over the surface of the sea, and the doomed hulk foundered. Although the collision took place ten miles off Barnegat Light, the ship's remains washed up on shore near the Bond's (Holgate) Life-Saving Station, on the southern end of Long Beach Island. The bodies of the Waltons, as well as those of the other two victims, were never found.

¤

BENEATH THE SHIFTING SANDS

The sandy shore of Long Beach Island, where the land meets the sea, is the burial ground for numerous wrecks. The shells and wooden skeletons of these seagoing behemoths repose for an eternity beneath the sand and, on occasion, are exhumed as the whim of the weather calls them to the surface.

As the first edition of this book was being written, a mysterious raft-like piece of ship was laid bare by an early winter storm. It rose as a ghost from beneath the powdery fringes of terra firma. Children danced on it, unknowing and uncaring about its origin.

Just beyond the dunes of 7th Street in Barnegat Light, the rusted spikes and crusted beams drew a parade of the curious. What great ship, or nameless barge, did it belong to? Was it a bulkhead, a deck, of one one of the lost ships of this volume?

Those who thought they might know could still, admittedly, only speculate. But lo, those who share the romance of the sea and of those who sail it, were drawn as if this wretched hulk was a magnet for the imagination.

Soon enough, this weathered shard returned to obscurity. Tides and tempests pushed the sand back, and interred the mysterious artifact until nature would be ready to reveal her prize once again in the future.

"Visible wrecks" are delineated on nautical charts, and are true tourist attractions at other shoal-ribbed capes and barrier islands. On Long Beach Island, there was an era when the washing up of ships to shore was not an uncommon occurrence.

Except for chunks of wrecks such as the one described above, and, of course, the mast that pokes out of the beach just south of Barnegat Lighthouse, the beaches here are devoid of such derelicts.

One of the most dramatic beachings of any ship on Long Beach Island was that of the Italian three-masted iron bark **Fortuna**, which rolled onto the beach near the Ship Bottom Life-Saving Station on January 18, 1910.

Heavy with coal bound to New York from Barbados, the bark carried thirteen crew men, Captain Luigi Andragna, his wife, and three children. One of those children was a newborn baby.

The ship was built in 1869 in Hamburg, Germany, and was operating out of Trapani, Sicily.

As the ship coasted along Long Beach Island, the weather turned seasonably foul. An icy wind kicked up, and rain and fog descended upon the helpless vessel. While the crew fought to maintain a course, the **Fortuna** drifted toward the beach.

Within minutes of the start of the fierce southeaster, the bark was hard aground, stranded within sight of the Ship Bottom station.

SHIPWRECKS NEAR BARNEGAT INLET

Captain Ike Truex of the Ship Bottom station believed at first that there was hope that little damage had been done and the ship could easily be pulled from the sands. The savage storm was relentless, and each gust drove her deeper into the bar and threatened the bark's watertight integrity.

A surfboat managed to row to the ship, and it was decided that all hands aboard would be taken off, as a precaution. Slowly but surely, each crewman and the captain and his family were hauled to shore via a breech buoy. Also saved, for the record, was a pig and a cat.

Still harboring hopes that the vessel could be tugged from the sand bar, the Merritt-Chapman Wrecking Company was requested along with the tug **Relief**. But, the storm had done its damage, and as the tides receded and the storm abated, it was determined that the **Fortuna** was a total loss.

Crowds of people from the shore gathered around as she was unceremoniously broken up for scrap.

Still, heavier parts of the **Fortuna** were relegated to a sandy grave.

In 1983, a Long Beach Island resident discovered several roofing tiles the ship was known to have been carrying. Then, that same individual found the actual three-ton anchor of the Fortuna in the sand.

The relic was preserved and put on exhibit at the entrance to the Ship Bottom town hall.

¤

The "Fortuna" wreck. Photo by Charles E. Nash. (Courtesy of the Barnegat Light Historical Museum)

37

THE BONE WRECK

The name conjures up weird thoughts.
"The Bone Wreck."
Actually, the "bone wreck" is so named for a very good reason.

The discovery of a mysterious bone, bleached white and smoothed as if by sandpaper, on a beach near Barnegat Inlet after a storm would not be unusual. It would be the signature of the wreck of the **Caterina**—the "bone wreck."

The three-masted Italian bark Caterina was once known as the **Formosa**. Built in Dumbarton in 1875, the iron-hulled, 860-ton vessel sailed under the ownership of Guiseppi Drago of Genoa, Italy, the day she went down.

It was October 23, 1912 when the **Caterina** was making way from Montevideo, Uruguay, to New York, with a cargo of bones which were to be ground up for fertilizer.

Coasting in a 30-knot gale, the ship was driven far off course and swept dangerously close to the Barnegat Shoals. Early in the evening of October 23, she was torn by those shoals.

SHIPWRECKS NEAR BARNEGAT INLET

A crew of 19 held on as the wind and sea battered the hulk. The wreck lay just offshore, but too far out for the Life-Saving Station crews to utilize their breech buoys. Thus, surf boats from the Forked River, Cedar Creek, Barnegat City and Loveladies stations gathered to come to the aid of the crew. The sea was so rough that the Italian crew men took to the rigging to await their fate.

That fate was kind, as the life-savers managed to fight the sea and use the tides to their advantage to make the rescue.

All crew members were brought safely ashore, detained overnight at the Forked River Life-Saving Station until the following, and taken to New York by train in the morning.

Offshore, however, there were efforts afoot to salvage the **Caterina**. The revenue cutter **Mohawk** from New York, came and attempted to pull the bark off the shoals, but to no avail. The gale-force winds and crashing sea proved indomitable foes.

The ship was a loss, and her cargo was washed away by the tide.

Today, this "bone wreck" is a seamark well known by fishermen and divers. Most of the wreck is blanketed by the sandy bottom, with the bow peeking out about 17 feet from the surface. Blackfish, tog and trigger fish, as well as small sea bass, have been known to frequent the site, and the wreck is a skin diver's delight. Water conditions are generally good, but can be quite the opposite, depending on any recent storm activity.

The wreck is about one-half mile northwest of the North Monument and less than one-half mile from the beach. Even today, bones occasionally churn up and wash ashore.

There is some element of confusion regarding the "bone wreck." Just nine years before the wreck of the **Caterina**, another bone-laden ship bound from South America (Buenos Aires) to New York spilled her cargo upon the beaches just south of Barnegat Light, near Surf City.

SHIPWRECKS NEAR BARNEGAT INLET

The officers of that three-masted, 1-605-ton ship were all well-educated Spaniards, in charge of a rather motley crew. It was a mixture of Malaysians, Filipinos, and what were described in contemporary accounts as Chinese "coolies." Their cargo was just as motley.

Her holds filled with bones destined to be fertilizer in the great farm fields of America, the **Remedios Pascual** sailed up the Jersey coast without incident until a "nor'easter" swept her close to the barrier islands. Valiantly, no doubt, the helmsman fought to prevent the inevitable, but the fury of the storm prevailed.

The ship was lost at 3:15 a.m., January 3, 1903. All hands were saved.

These "bone wrecks" of Barnegat Inlet and of Surf City are certainly not the glamorous shipwrecks one may find in the Florida Keys or the shoals of the Caribbean. A blanched animal bone does not compare in intrinsic value to a Gold Doubloon.

Still, there is an air of mysterious surrounding the thought, and indeed the name, "Bone Wreck." And yes, even a pathetic bone, given up by the stingy sea, can be a treasure on the beach of Long Beach Island.

✡

*In an ironic twist of fate, the **Mohawk**, sent to rescue the **Caterina**, was itself a shipwreck victim in 1917.*

The 980-ton U.S. Treasury Department "Revenue Cutter" was pressed into service patrolling New York harbor during World War I.

*While on guard in the Ambrose Channel as convoys plied the busy shipping lanes, the British freighter **Vennachar** smashed into the cutter midships, sending the **Mohawk** to the bottom.*

*The cutter's 77-man crew was rescued safely by the U.S.S. **Mohican** and U.S.S. **Sabalo**.*

40

THE GALES OF DECEMBER

If, as folk singer Gordon Lightfoot said in his incredible "Wreck of the Edmund Fitzgerald," the mariners of Lake Superior know of the furious "gales of November" on the Great Lakes, the sea off Long Beach Island must lay claim to the "gales of December."

The frolicking summertime day trippers and part-time islanders up and down Long Beach Island can scarcely imagine the tempestuous winters in these parts.

The same ocean that tickles the body surfers and washes gently over sand castles in the warm afternoons of August transforms into a killing sea that has claimed untold lives and ships.

Two victims of this rage were, in their primes, noble ladies of the sea. Students of maritime history will likely recall the name, **A.G. Ropes**, whenever the golden age of sail is mentioned. A handsome "down east'r" built in the legendary Bath, Maine, shipyards of Ropes and Chapman,

41

SHIPWRECKS NEAR BARNEGAT INLET

The **A.G. Ropes** was a magnificent three-masted schooner capable of making some of the fastest New York-to-San Francisco voyages possible at that time.

That time was the second half of the nineteenth century, when graceful clippers such as the **Henry B. Hyde** and the **A.G. Ropes** competed on the "great tea race" runs.

Big money was often bet on the **Ropes**, which eventually set a new N.Y.-S.F. record, completing her assignment in 93 days.

In her 29 years of mighty sailing history, the **A.G. Ropes** could turn an average of 6.5 knots and in 1885-86, she finished the mightiest voyage of her proud career. In a remarkable 208 days, she sailed from San Francisco to Europe, back to New York, and on again to the Golden Gate!

The **A.G. Ropes** fell victim to the maritime revolution of the late nineteenth century. Wood was giving way to iron, sail to steam, and the **A.G. Ropes'** vaunted service was nearing its end.

Still, she was a hardy vessel. Her 258-foot long hull, measuring more than 44 feet at the beam, was still serviceable as a barge, and in 1906, she was purchased by Lewis Luckenbach for such use. Luckenbach had, six years prior, converted another solid Bath-built clipper, the **Undaunted**, into a towing vessel. The **Undaunted** had, too, a noteworthy 31 years of service on the high seas.

Exactly what happened on that frigid day after Christmas, 1913, when the two barges collided sending ten men into the drink will never be truly known. There are disparaging reports from crew men, and for many months the tale of the wreck was popular fodder in the taverns and fishermen's shacks of the area.

No one aboard either barge lived to tell their side of the story, so all that was left after the rumors and speculation settled was a final report which absolved the tug crew men of any wrongdoing. The crew of the tug, Edgar Luckenbach, were finally unified in their version, saying the hawser between the tug and the barges snagged on a fishpound piling, sending the barges and their ten men adrift.

There were those who raised eyebrows as the story related was related by the tugmen. They whispered doubts that a fishpound piling could ever snap a hawser. More realistic, said the doubters, was the theory that the crew men of the tug, being swamped by the December gale, decided they could ride out the storm better without their burden. Perhaps they warned the barge crews of their intentions and told them to drop anchor and wait out the storm. No anchor could have performed the feat needed to keep the barges from dashing ashore.

From Long Beach Island, observers could see the tug and her two encumberments struggling against the heavy seas and fierce wind. It appeared that the storm was driving all three vessels beachward toward Seaside Park. Heavily laden with coal bound from Philadelphia to Providence, the barges were helpless derelicts once the hawser was severed—by whatever means.

The raging sea toppled the barges about one-half mile offshore, some seven miles south of Seaside Park. Nine of the ten men who perished were swept away instantly, but one man who lashed himself to the rigging of one of the barges managed to survive a mite longer.

Life-Saving crew members from the Forked River station saw the man's valiant struggle against insurmountable odds, and fought the sea in an attempt to save him. They radioed for help from the "revenue" (the predecessor of the Coast Guard) and hoped a cutter would arrive in time to help.

Their hopes were crushed as the waves buried the barge, and the sole survivor, in one final surge.

Even though the life-savers gave their all, they knew inside that the figure lashed to the rigging of the barge was probably nothing more than a corpse by the time they came close enough to be of assistance.

When the storm subsided and the sea calmed, the

tragedy was reviewed. Lost were ten men, including O. Olson and William Fickett, captains of the barges. The tug's master, Captain C.T. Knight, kept his vessel in the area in an attempt to aid the barge crews, but that proved hopeless.

The barges sank in about 25 feet of water, and what was left of them eventually washed up on shore very close to the Forked River Life-Saving Station.

The "revenue" cutter **Onondaga** searched for bodies following the wreck, but none was ever found. A contemporary news account of the incident said, "It is assumed that the bodies may have drifted to sea and they may come to shore far away."

Only the dreaded "Davey Jones" knows where, and if ever.

¤

THE KILLER WAVE

The wind and the waves bore down on the beaches like an angry fist, beating and bashing all in the way. Homes became match sticks, snapped and crushed at will by the hurricane-force fury.

Bulkheads along the shore buckled under the intense pressure. The land was swept clean as if by a giant broom.

It was January 4, 1914, Long Beach Island, New Jersey.

The winter had not been kind to the island. For the second time within the same week, the testy North Atlantic had reared its ugly head.

The long and heavy tanker, **Oklahoma**, was bloated. Her 419-foot, 5,795-ton frame was filled with crude oil. She was a bone to be chewed by the vicious jowls of the tempest.

Barely six years at sea, the Camden-built ship was under the command of Captain Albert Gunther. A few days before the **Oklahoma's** appointment with destiny, her sister ship had escaped a similar fate in the week's first storm.

This time, the sea was to claim another victim. The ship was rigged for heavy seas and all precautions were being taken for an anticipated safe passage through the storm of January 4.

The waves pounded the **Oklahoma**. Her steel plates growled and groaned until they could stand no more. A massive wave swept over her decks, battering her into submission. With an unimaginable thrust, the wave snapped the massive vessel in two.

The storm had knocked out any hope of

45

communication with the life-saving stations on Long Beach or Island Beach. The **Oklahoma** was some seven miles northeast of Barnegat, beyond the realistic reach of any shore help, even if it could have been summoned.

There was little hope. Of the 38 men aboard the tanker, most drowned in the stern section, which sank almost immediately after the killer wave struck.

On the bow section, there was life. The swift current swept the bow section southward, with Captain Gunther and seven crew members aboard. The ship's distress call was received by at least five other vessels in the area, and shortly after the destruction of the **Oklahoma**, the steamships **Caribbean, Bavaria, Manuel Calvo, Gregory, Tenodores,** and the revenue cutter **Seneca** all arrived to render assistance.

At first, the ships surrounding the **Oklahoma** did not know her identity. But no matter, the primary concern was to search for survivors on that stormy Sunday morning.

The steamer **Bavaria**, en route from Hamburg, Germany, to Philadelphia, picked up eight survivors who rode the bow section to salvation. Exhausted from exposure, they nonetheless were lucky to be alive.

The hopes for any other survivors were grim. The waves surely would have consumed any other souls on any lesser flotsam than the bow of the tanker. Miraculously, however, this was not the case!

Aboard the Booth Line steamship **Gregory**, lookouts noticed a half-sunken lifeboat being tossed about in the storm. Aboard it were the half-dead figures of several men.

Almost by instinct, three officers from the **Gregory**, clad in their foul-weather gear, plunged into the frenzied foam. They battled the sea and grabbed three bodies. Two of the men lived, but the third could not be revived.

The brave men from the **Gregory**, defying all odds, tied a line to the ravaged lifeboat and the boat with its precious human cargo was pulled to the steamship.

There were other lifeboats sent out by the **Oklahoma** in

her dying gasps, but all aboard these were washed overboard.

The drama continued for hours. In all, a dozen men from the **Oklahoma** lived to tell their stories. Two dozen of their shipmates did not.

The bow section of the **Oklahoma** remained afloat, defiantly challenging the sea that had severed it from its stern. The cutter **Seneca**, whose mission was to destroy derelict vessels, was assigned to chase down the bow portion. It did so, but not until after it had floated a good distance from where the stern had sunk.

In fact, the forward portion of the ship continued to drift almost 100 miles south. On January 8, the **Seneca** found a mysterious piece of ship floating off the coast of Maryland.

The **Seneca** gunners poured 20 rounds of their six-pounders into the hulk. The stubborn stub of a ship rolled over, clearly exposing its nameplate. It was the bow of the **Oklahoma**.

Today, the two sections are far apart, nestled on the bottom of the ocean.

¤

THE MYSTERY OF
THE CEDAR CREEK WRECK

There is, in the wreck charts of the Jersey coasts, an anonymous pile of ocean-floor rubble known as "The Cedar Creek Wreck."

Located nearly six miles from the North Monument and about a mile from shore, the charts lack any substantive information about the type of vessel, or when and by what means it was sent to the depths.

It could very well be, then, that "The Cedar Creek Wreck" may indeed be that of the **Charlemagne Tower Jr.**, a wooden steam freighter that broke apart in rough seas at about 7 a.m., March 6, 1914.

Built in a Great Lakes shipbuilding facility in 1886, the **Charlemagne Tower Jr.** was of 1,544 net and 3,000 gross tons, and carried a cargo of coal to New England. The 255-foot steamer boasted oak decks and was, in her prime, one of the workhorses of the Southern Steamship Company.

By the time of her sinking, however, she was victimized by engine troubles, malfunctioning equipment, and had begun to strain after 28 years of hard service.

On March 4, 1914, the captain, a man named Murphy, set sail with a crew of 17 from Norfolk to Boston with the ship's belly gorged with "black gold." Within hours of departure from Tidewater, however, there were problems in the engine room. Captain Murphy elected to return and put in at Hampton Roads for the necessary repairs. A few hours later, the problems were corrected and the ship left once again for her ultimate destination, the New England Coal Company.

Such mechanical troubles were not new to the **Charlemagne Tower Jr.**. The ship lay in mothballs for about six years before she was pressed into service a few weeks prior to her sinking.

Hints that something was wrong began to be noticed the day after the ship set sail the second time. The wireless equipment was failing, and the violent waves tossed the ship incessantly upon the ocean surface.

By the dawn of March 6, there was fear that the ship would not reach Boston. The fears of the captain and crew were realized when the bottom seams of the hull opened and water started to rush in. By 9 a.m., the ship was filled with sea water to the beams.

Captain Murphy gave the order to abandon ship, and with 13 other men, boarded a longboat. Three other men put out on a smaller lifeboat.

The frigid North Atlantic quickly took its toll on the men. There was a small sail on the longboat, but the men were too cold to hoist it. The seas were far too rough for sailing.

Because the collier's radio room had eventually flooded out, crewmen desperately scrawled flags which alerted anyone who would see: *WE ARE SINKING. SEND LIFE BOATS.*

While the **Charlemagne Tower Jr.** was in her death throes, another ship, the Old Dominion steamer **Hamilton**, came near. Captain Nelson of the **Hamilton** later told an inquiry board that he brought his ship close enough to the **Charlemagne Tower Jr.** to read its name on the bow, saw no evidence of life on board, radioed its position identifying it as a derelict vessel, and continued on his course.

Captain Murphy accused Captain Nelson of neglecting the distress call of the ill-fated ship. Whatever the case, life-saving station personnel on shore were alerted by the radio call from the **Hamilton** and put out to have a look.

The three crew men aboard the lifeboat made it to shore with the help of the surfmen. The other fourteen survivors were rescued by a passing vessel later in the evening, all suffering from frostbite and covered with snow.

Today, the wreck of the **Charlemagne Tower Jr.** rests with 36 feet of water over it. And, that mysterious wreckage known as "The Cedar Creek Wreck" may be that of the collier that broke apart and sank that wretched morning in 1914.

It is one of the most interesting wrecks along the New Jersey shore, in that it was built on the lines of a classic Great Lakes ore carrier.

Its pilot house is propped over the prow, and the engine house is under the fantail.

¤

THE SHIPWRECK
WITHOUT A THRILL

The title is not ours.

We borrow it from a contemporary newspaper article in which the writer labeled the wreck of the **Sumner** as such because there was no loss of life, the ship went aground with a gentle heave in soft sand, and help scurried to the scene within minutes.

It is true that many of the wrecks in the approaches to Barnegat Inlet do not have the magnitude of, say, the **R.M.S. Titanic** or the **Andrea Doria**. Nor do they capture the public's (or the media's) fancy as did the romantic wrecks of the Florida Keys and West Indies.

Still, they are the stuff of which this stretch of coastline is all about. Even if there was no death, and cargo of the **Sumner** was only 800 tons of scrap iron, it and other ships that have come and gone merit a mention in this log of the sea.

For many years, the **Sumner's** seagoing carcass was visible on the beaches of Barnegat Light. Dismembered chunks of metal lay in the sands, and they were occasionally bared by the shifting and drifting of the seafront. Like quicksand, the beach sucked the scraps deeper until now there is no evidence, nothing to remind anyone of the **Sumner** and its last night at sea on Monday, December 12, 1916.

The 351-foot, 3,458-ton U.S. Army transport ship was built in Hamburg, Germany, in 1888, and christened as the **Rhaetia**.

51

SHIPWRECKS NEAR BARNEGAT INLET

The U.S. Navy purchased her in 1899 and put her into service as the coal-carrying **U.S.S. Cassius.**

Later, she was refitted and reassigned to the U.S. Army to serve the nation that would go to war against the country in which it was launched.

The **Sumner** left Colon, Panama, on December 4 with numerous government employees, troops and crew men aboard.

The passenger list included eleven women and eight children under five years of age. All aboard were saved when the ship ran aground in sixteen feet of water, at high tide, about 300 yards from Barnegat City.

For Captain B.E. Webber, the **Sumner** was to be a memorable command. But not, he hoped, for the reason of the grounding. It was his very first command, and he hoped to work his way through the ranks. It is questionable whether Webber, who obviously allowed the ship to run aground because of careless navigation, ever received another ship's command.

There was little moonlight at midnight when the ship swept onto the shore. Ships in the vicinity monitored the distress call. The **Sumner's** wireless operator radioed that he suspected the vessel may have been aground. He could hear the surf breaking against the side of the ship, but it was too dark to confirm.

Soon, another message.

Distress!

S.O.S.!

The **Sumner** *had* run aground, and was resting easily in light sand. In the inky middle of the night, it was impossible to tell that the ship was in but sixteen feet of water, and was so close to the shore.

The distress calls sent life-saving crews and other ships to the scene. The steamers **Themisiocies** and **City of Montgomery** rendezvoused to offer aid, and the Coast Guard cutter **Mohawk** steamed to the scene. They knew not what they would find, and the drama heightened when the **Sumner's** radio operator's last message was received: *"S.O.S....S.O.S....WE ARE LAUNCHING POW--....."*

The radio was dead.

Could the **Sumner**, her crew and her passengers have met a hideous fate?

Actually, all but a midnight watch were asleep aboard the **Sumner** at the time of the grounding. The "wreck without a thrill" was so uneventful at the time that none of the passengers was even shaken awake.

Until daybreak, the **Sumner** rested embarrassingly in the breaking surf. The wrecking tug **Tasco** from Newport, Rhode Island, and a counterpart from Norfolk, Virginia, were summoned to pull the big ship from the sands.

As the **Sumner** wallowed, her bow pointing north and a dangerous starboard list imperiling her stability, the surf began to take its toll. The waves rocked the ship, sending her scrap-iron cargo tumbling willy-nilly in the holds. The heavy freight buried the ship deeper and deeper, making the tugs' job unenviable.

For six days, the tugs pulled in an effort to free the vessel. The iron was unloaded in an effort to lighten the ship. Still, the sea pushed and shoved against its bulkheads. Finally, the ship began to break apart. One of the tugs ripped the rudder from the hull and damaged the stern section. The 28-year old craft was about to perish.

The **Sumner's** crew remained aboard throughout the attempts of salvage. The passengers, however, were escorted off the ship, after their rude awakening the morning after the beaching.

Even for those who retired that fateful night, there was little reason to believe they would wake up a stone's thrown from land the next morning. Seas were calm, the ship was steaming at about half speed, and all had seemed to be well.

If there were any "thrills" at all surrounding this debacle, they were reserved for the passengers and the befuddled U.S. Customs agents who greeted them once they were trained to New York. As it turned out, however, only a few of those who were brought ashore by the Coast Guard arrived on the special train. Puzzled Customs agents, always seeking to do a complete and thorough job, were forced to find the remaining survivors.

Those folks, the Customs men found, had been transported to Manhattan aboard the cutter **Mohawk**.

The rescue of the passengers from the **Sumner** was not without incident, however insignificant it may seem now.

Women passengers complained they were getting wet climbing down the rope ladder. The ladder was also about six feet too short, so those disembarking the ship were forced to jump into the lifeboats. There were no injuries. No thrills.

So, the "shipwreck without a thrill" story ended quietly and, alas, without a thrill.

But it would be a thrill for any beachcomber who, someday after a storm, may walk along the beach at Barnegat Light and see, emerging from the sand like a long-buried treasure, a remnant of the **Sumner**.

Sometimes, you have to wait a long, long time for a thrill!

¤

THE WRECK OF THE CHAPARRA

A tale of human compassion and, perhaps, superhuman strength highlights the tragedy of the Cuban freighter, **Chaparra**.

The 1,505-ton vessel was on its way from Cuba to the Federal Sugar Refining Company of New York City with 2,000 tons of raw sugar from the fields of the Caribbean island.

Fifteen crew men, under their master, Captain Jose Vinslas, were enjoying an uneventful cruise up the coast, ever wary of the possibility that their seaborne solitude could be interrupted at any time by the Kaiser's "unterseeboots" that reportedly plied the same busy merchant lines.

It was Sunday evening, October 27, 1918, when the **Chaparra** passed over the position that, about a month earlier, had proven to be the final resting spot of the Mallory freighter, **San Saba**. Perhaps the crew knew and took note of this harbinger. Perhaps not.

The silence of the sea was shattered abruptly and, for the **Chaparra**, forever, that night when the ship's bow steamed directly into a mine, presumably planted by a German submarine, **U-117**.

Explosions rocked the vessel. Six men were killed instantly and within five minutes the **Chaparra** was headed toward its watery grave.

Nine crew members managed to scurry from the rapidly-sinking freighter and made it to a lifeboat in the five minutes the **Chaparra** took to slip beneath the waves. To the ocean floor, some 75 feet below, the ship descended. It

55

finally struck bottom just fifty feet from the remains of the **San Saba**, some 7.4 miles from the North Monument of the New Jersey coast.

For what seemed an eternity, the nine men crowded aboard the lifeboat hoped, seemingly against hope, that the waves would drift them to the shore. They struggled to stay alive, and to paddle their way to the beach. The beckoning light of Barnegat provided some guidance and, in the end, proved to be their salvation.

The heroics of the lighthouse keepers up and down the coasts of the world are often lost in non-recorded history. Occasionally, a story of incredible resolve and rescue surfaces, and provides a realistic glimpse of the dedication and courage of these men and women.

Such is the case of the wife of Frank Thompson, the assistant keeper of Barnegat Light.

Doubtlessly, the woman on watch at "Old Barney" on that fateful night in October, 1918, saw the flash of the explosion and the glow of the fire as the **Chaparra** met its fate on the horizon.

For hours, she kept a close watch as whatever moonlight there may have been and whatever kind of light her lifebeam could provide danced of the pounding waves.

She would watch...listen...hope...that a small craft would be spotted, and survivors could be saved.

Sure enough, her surfside vigilance proved positive, as the tiny lifeboat was finally seen drifting toward shore. But by that time, the crew men were near delirium, ravaged by their ordeal and frightfully unable to bring the boat through the breakers.

The sailors were just a few yards from safety, but the incoming waves refused to allow them to beach their battered vessel. Mrs. Thompson, defying the cold of a late-October ocean, waded waist deep into the Atlantic, pointed the bow of the boat toward the shore, and pulled the men to a safe refuge.

56

LOST IN THE FOG

The fog off the coast of Long Beach Island on February 17, 1927 was said to be the most dense in several years.

Doubtlessly, many vessels inched their way through the shroud, up and down the coastline, with no incidents.

But, for the 1,216-ton **Cecil P. Stewart**, out of Rockland, Maine, the thick fog proved to be its undoing.

Just eight years at sea, the **Stewart** was laden with railroad ties bound from Brunswick, Georgia, to New York. She carried minimum sail and all crew men were on lookout as the fog enveloped her in a blinding blanket of white.

She drew 18 feet, and a lead line was dropped to feel the bottom. Like a childish tickler poking between ribs, the line gauged the undulating underwater bars just offshore.

"A few minutes before three o'clock, I got my first fair reckoning and knew that we were edging landward," Captain Edward Fale told reporters that night. "The lead line showed decreasing water. I had barely given the order to throw her about when we struck."

57

SHIPWRECKS NEAR BARNEGAT INLET

The vessel cracked against the sandbar. crew men struggled to stay upright. Rough seas tumbled over her vulnerable and doomed decks.

Frantically, the crew hastened to the cabin tops and shrouds and fired distress signals. The thick fog continued to be the nemesis of the men of the **Cecil P. Stewart**. Even the flares shot by the crew could not penetrate the fog. Vigilant life-savers less than a mile away at Harvey Cedars were oblivious to the plight of the **Stewart**.

Finally, the fog lifted and the distress signals were sighted. It was about 6:30, some three and one-half hours after the grounding of the ship, when the first life boat was pushed into the surf.

As the drama unfolded, crews from Barnegat City, Loveladies and Ship Bottom stations joined their compatriots at Harvey Cedars to facilitate the rescue.

The task was no easy one. The first boat plunged into the heavy breakers and was nearly swamped several times. Still, four crew men managed to leap into the smallboat.

A second boat made it to the Stewart at eight o'clock, about five harrowing hours after the ship struck the bar. Again, the ocean tossed her about like a small bottle. This time, the captain and four crew men were taken aboard as the **Cecil P. Stewart** rapidly deteriorated.

Waves smashed into the ship's starboard side and eventually split her seams open. There was no hope for salvage.

The **Stewart** was built and rigged as a bark, but was later converted into a schooner. Her cargo of tarred railroad ties contributed greatly to her demise, splitting her open from within as the seas outside did the rest.

The ship gradually broke up and parts washed onto the shore at Harvey Cedars. About all that was salvageable from the broken ship were the railroad ties. Long Beach Island scavengers huckstered these prizes at a half-dollar apiece. Still today, perhaps, these bulky wooden ties grace island properties, fulfilling their destinies.

Years of seaside changes eventually buried the remains of the **Stewart** far into the sands. But in 1936 and 1937, a series of violent storms raked the Harvey Cedars area, and bared the skeleton of the schooner for all to see.

The reverse action of the never-ending cycle of a beach's life has, however, once again entombed the beams of the **Cecil P. Stewart** beneath the sand.

¤

The keel-section of the schooner "Cecil P. Stewart" as it appeared after the raging storms of 1936-37. (Photo by Charles E. Nash, courtesy of Barnegat Light Hist. Soc.)

59

LOST AND PRESUMED DROWNED

The title of this tale sets the stage for the stormy story of the loss of the schooner barges **Arkansas** *(or Aransas, in some references)* and **Cogensville** on January 28, 1928.

The tug **Baldrock**, under the command of Captain Robert Parker, was towing the two ill-fated barges and another barge, the **Nahant**, from Norfolk, Virginia to Kearny, New Jersey. All three barges were riding deep with cargoes of coal.

The fickle January weather took a turn for the worst when a storm brewed just off the Barnegat Shoals. Captain Parker of the **Baldrock** valiantly fought the odds, as the hawsers strained with each surge of the sea.

These vital umbilical cords were tested to their limits. Aboard the barges, crew men must have known they were in peril.

Captain Ira Parker of the **Cogensville** and Captain Harvey Twilley aboard the **Arkansas** were still virtually powerless. Their fate, and the fates of the men aboard the barges, rested almost entirely with the strength of the lifelines that attached their vessels to the mother ship.

The strength of those lifelines was sapped by the choppy seas and the 1,300-ton loads of both barges. The two helpless crafts broke loose, while the **Nahant** remained connected.

Knowing full well that any kind of rescue attempt at the time would be dangerously impossible, the tug steamed northward with its sole surviving encumbrance. The Coast Guard was unaware of the tragedy, and could therefore offer no aid.

The **Baldrock** made a quick turnaround in New York harbor and returned to search the area where the barges drifted away from the tug. The lives of eight men aboard the barges were already conceded. There was no hope of finding any survivors, unless by some miracle the barges managed to stay afloat.

When the **Baldrock** arrived at the position of the loss, the crew's worst fears were realized. All that was left was a ghostly sight.

The masts of the barges poked out of the waves, bony fingers beckoning unwary sailors into the deep.

No wreckage, no bodies drifted ashore. As more winter storms raked the seas, the ravaged wrecks of the **Arkansas** and **Cogensville** rapidly broke apart underwater. Over a period of time, the masts slowly sank beneath the waves.

The Eastern Transportation Company of Boston, owners of the barges, estimated the loss at $84,000 per barge. But what they could not estimate, and indeed what no man can ever reckon, was the human toll.

Lost...and presumed drowned.

¤

A WAR OF WORDS

Although we know that Nazi submarines in notorious "wolf packs" patrolled America's east coast during World War II and there was considerable disruption of maritime shipping, not all of the "war" involved mines, torpedoes and bullets.

The American freighter, **Lillian**, rests on the ocean floor, some 140 feet below the surface, as mute testimony to a dramatic episode between herself and the German freighter **Wiegand**.

The collision between the two vessels on a foggy night in February, 1939, touched off a war of words between the captains and crews of the two ships. Anti-German sentiment, building stronger in the United States at the time, may have played a role in the charges and counter-charges leveled in the aftermath.

This is not a tragic tale of human agony. All 32 of those aboard the **Lillian** were plucked from the sea following the ship's demise. It is, more than anything, a tale of confusion and anguish between two principals that would, within a few years, become mortal enemies.

The fog was thick as the two ships approached a point about fifteen miles northeast of Barnegat Inlet. The **Lillian** was loaded with an estimated $400,000 worth of raw sugar bound from Puerto Rico to New York. Her 238-foot bulk displaced 3,482 tons, and she was operated by the American "Bull Line."

The German ship was lumbering through the fog, heavily laden with a cargo of scrap iron being transported from Brooklyn to Moji, Japan. The 370-foot freighter was manned by 48 sailors and displaced 6,568 tons.

SHIPWRECKS NEAR BARNEGAT INLET

Captain Frank C. Boyer of the **Lillian** was feeling his way through the dense fog, sounding his ship's foghorn every sixty to ninety seconds, conforming with international navigational regulations.

Or, so he said.

Captain Leopold Ranitz, master of the Lloyd Lines freighter from Germany, said his ship was steaming slowly through the fog. As the murk thickened, speed was reduced.

Nine knots...seven knots...five knots....

Slower and slower.

Water was breaking over the giant ship's bow. There was no lookout aloft, Captain Ranitz said, because there was nothing to be seen in the "soup" that engulfed the ship. Still, from the bridge, all precautions were taken.

Or, so he said.

Whatever the true circumstances, the **Lillian** and **Wiegand** struck at about 7 p.m., February 6, 1939. The **Lillian** plowed into the **Wiegand** with such force that plates of her side were driven through the forecastle and out the other side, from starboard to port.

7:12 p.m: "S.O.S.....S.O.S.....S.O.S."

The fatal message was tapped out on the **Lillian's** wireless. There was little doubt. The American freighter was doomed.

The radio operator reported the ship would probably sink within fifteen minutes.

"S.O.S....S.O.S."

The operator stayed at his post. Water was rushing into the radio shack.

"S.O.S....S.O.S."

Radioman William Helmbold, who was later praised for his actions, remained. Frantically, as water washed over his ankles, he tapped it out.

"DOT, DOT, DOT...DASH, DASH, DASH...DOT, DOT, DOT!"

Finally, he saw that the worse was imminent, so he

locked his wireless key so it would send a continuous signal. Someone, somewhere, would hear and would save his, and his shipmates' lives.

All told, Helmbold remained at his post for about an hour. The order to abandon ship came at 8:07 p.m., and the final message monitored was *We are getting ready to abandon ship....So-long, and I guess I will get my feet wet!*

Helmbold's estimate that the **Lillian** would go down in about fifteen minutes was well off the mark. She foundered for hours, giving the crew ample time to abandon her in a fairly orderly manner. Some crew men sustained rope burns while lowering the lifeboats. Captain Boyer sprained his back dropping to a lifeboat.

Searchlights from the **Wiegand** pierced the fog, revealing choppy but manageable seas. The German freighter sounded her whistle so the men on the **Lillian's** lifeboats could judge their range and distance.

From the first S.O.S. sent from the **Lillian**, the Coast Guard cutter **Campbell** and the American steamer **Munmotor** hastened to the area.

8:39 p.m., **Munmotor** to **Wiegand**: *We will be there in about thirty minutes. Have you picked them up yet?*

8:44 p.m., **Wiegand** to **Munmoter**: *One with seventeen men rescues. Expecting second boat with rest of crew.*

There was a deceptive silence for several minutes, and then...

9:21 p.m., from the **Wiegand**: *Second boat with rest of crew coming alongside.*

9:27 p.m., from the **Wiegand**: *No further assistance needed. Rescue is completed.*

The **Lillian** sank slowly. By the middle of the night, she was still struggling to remain afloat. And by that time, a small flotilla had rallied around the stricken steamer. Because the vessel seemed to defy the lure of Neptune, there was a glimmer of hope that she may be salvaged. First, however, there was a small matter to be taken care of by the Coast Guard.

There was no doubt that wireless operator Helmbold's deeds were meritorious, but the telegraph key he locked into position was still locked. The incessant signal jammed the channel. Coast Guardsman tried to pull close to the **Lillian**, hoping to board her and release the key. The seas were too choppy, so they did the next best thing—they shot off the antenna!

The act turned out to be the coup de grace for the **Lillian**. The salvage ship that eyed her from afar, in hopes of plucking her from the grip of Davey Jones, got to within a bout one hundred yards of the listing hulk when the **Lillian** rolled to the depths.

Captain Boyer and sixteen crew men from the **Lillian** had gathered on board the Coast Guard boat **Icarus** to assist in any possible salvage effort. They watched silently as the steel behemoth that served as their workplace and home for so very long disappeared forever.

For Captain Boyer, the sinking of his ship was but one chapter in a book of problems that had, perhaps, not yet reached its climax.

The crews of the German and American ships were men of the sea. There is an arbitrary "code" among such men. But still, sentiment and politics were at a fever pitch in 1939, and the level of tolerance had dropped, even in the seafaring fraternity.

The Wiegand had remained at the scene and had rendered assistance. Responding to a lamp signal from the **Lillian** advising the **Wiegand** that the American ship was in peril, the German vessel stayed.

She accepted the survivors and even transported them back to New York, where the **Wiegand** was to undergo repairs to a twelve-foot gash in her bow above the water line.

As hospitable and conciliatory as the two crews may have been on the high seas, they were just as hostile and combative in the ensuing days on shore.

The United States government called for an investigation into the collision. In one day, the testimony reached the boiling point, with both captains hurling responsibility for the incident at one another.

The morning session of the investigation saw Captain Ranitz blaming, in no uncertain terms, the **Lillian** for the crash. He claimed the American freighter came out of the fog with no warning.

He said there were no audible or visible signals. by the time the **Lillian** was visible from the bridge of the **Wiegand**, it was too late. The chief officer on the bridge at the time of the collision, Ludwig Klugkish, corroborated the captain's story.

That afternoon, the master of the **Lillian** was called to the stand. He promptly refuted the German's charges. Captain Boyer said his ship was following regulations, and the **Wiegand** was not. He said he heard no signals from the German craft, and when the **Wiegand** emerged from the fog, he ordered full astern. The thrust of the **Lillian** carried her into the side of the **Wiegand**.

After hearing both sides, the board of inquiry took what could be called the "easy way out." In all fairness, there was little else it could do. It was a classic case of "one man's word against the other's."

Both ships were at fault. The investigation concluded that both were steaming at excessive speeds (the **Lillian** at some 8.2 knots, too fast for fog) and the collision could have been avoided had both reduced their velocity.

The federal government acted to discipline Captain Frank Boyer. No doubt, they would have chosen to punish Captain Leopold Ranitz, also. But, the American authorities had no jurisdiction over the German master.

And do it was over. There was no loss of life, no serious injuries. Another ship went to the bottom and the lives of dozens of men were irretrievably altered.

SHIPWRECKS NEAR BARNEGAT INLET

How could they ever have dreamed how the lives of millions more men and women in their two homelands–and around the world–would be changed in the next few years?

¤

THE NAZIS SINK THE GULFTRADE

The harsh realities of World War II came fearfully close to the New Jersey coastline.

German U-Boats patrolled the shipping lanes and were responsible for the destruction of many ships, untold thousands of tons of cargo and hundreds of lives.

One victim of this sea war was the steam tanker **Gulftrade**. It now lies broken at the bottom of the Atlantic, a scant twelve miles from the North Monument.

At 4,223 net and 6,776 gross tons, the **GULFTRADE** was an ample ship, black-hulled with red boot topping. Her masts and derricks were a bright white, and even with the very distant threat of attack by the unseen enemy below, she chose to run with masthead and range light glaring.

Built in Chester, Pa. and home-ported in New York, the **GULFTRADE** was a sixteen-year veteran of coastal sailing on March 10, 1942, her last day. The ship was carrying 81,222 barrels of bunker "C" fuel oil from Venezuela to America when she met her fate.

The **GULFTRADE** was steaming at about 10.5 knots when a torpedo from the German sub **U-588** ripped through her hull, setting off a chain of explosions and fires that ravaged her from bow to stern, causing her to break in two.

The explosions demolished the radio room, so no distress calls could be sent out.[1]

In a frantic attempt to save themselves, sixteen of the crew members scurried to lifeboats and left the doomed hulk. Eighteen of their mates, fearing that the German sub would surface and gun them down, elected to stay on the burning

68

tanker. Only the Almighty knows how they met their deaths that dismal day in March.

Captain Torger Olsen reported that flames shot out of his vessel nearly 100 feet into the sky. Residents in Barnegat Light said they could easily see the burning ship.

Survivors say the sub did surface some five minutes after its attack, and after watching the spoils of his efforts, the captain of the sub circled the slowly-sinking, shattered inferno and steered a southerly course to seek more prey.

The Coast Guard boat **Antietam** was less than a mile from the **GULFTRADE** when the torpedo struck.

As the **Antietam** moved in to rescue any survivors, a lookout on the Coast Guard vessel reported a torpedo crossing less than 50 feet from the bow of his boat.

The bow and stern parts of the ship drifted apart as the seas tossed them and swirled them to the bottom, some fifty feet below.

Currents and drifts have separated the two portions of the sunken ship even more under the sea. The remains of the **GULFTRADE** now rest some five miles apart on the ocean floor.

Fuel in the stern tanks of the ship was salvaged, and portions of both the bow and stern of the 423-foot vessel have been dynamited to alleviate any navigational hazards.

¤

NAZIS "INVADE"
LONG BEACH ISLAND

The Nazi threat came closer to Long Beach Island than the distance the island is from the mainland. Casualties from this "attack" met their fates well within sight of Barnegat Light.

The big tanker **Persephone**, carrying fuel oil from Aruba to New York, was sailing in fair weather on May 25, 1942. She was the last ship in a convoy which was headed north along the coast.

It was wartime. There was airborne and seagoing protection afforded the merchant flotilla. But a daring Nazi U-Boat captain defied all the odds and decided the **Persephone** was easy pickings.

The master of the **Persephone**, Captain Helge Quistgaard, was in his cabin at two minutes until three in the afternoon as the 36 other men in his crew were about their business aboard the 8,426-ton giant.

Lookouts were posted, and all proper security measures were being taken by the Coast Guard. Even though the convoy was passing a scant 2.5 miles from the lighthouse at Barnegat Inlet, there was a real fear that the unterseeboots could penetrate and strike silently, without warning.

These fears were realized when a German torpedo ripped through the hull of the **Persephone**, catching all completely by surprise.

A blanket of black smoke enveloped the ship within seconds. The powerful torpedo drove deeply into the engine room on the ship's starboard side.

The crew scrambled.

World War II had smacked them squarely in their faces.

There was barely enough time to sort matters out before another underwater bullet burst through the starboard side again, this time into an oil tank, sending the black ooze gushing over the ship.

The stern of the **Persephone** shuddered and began to slip under the waves. The bow section, from the midship house forward, poked out of the water.

Captain Quistgaard shuffled to the bridge and immediately ordered the ship abandoned. Some crew members, quietly sipping coffee in the mess hall, were shaken by the explosions and managed to leap onto a raft to safety. Others found their way to a lifeboat and rowed away from the doomed ship.

Coast Guard vessels were on their way to the site. The **Persephone's** master rummaged through the ship and gathered up salvageable navigational instruments after he realized the ship was a loss. He lowered another lifeboat and became the sole passenger aboard it. He and 27 other survivors, were picked up by the cutter within minutes of the sinking. Nine of their mates were killed.

The Coast Guard ship and others in the area attempted to chase the submarine, but the stealthy U-Boat eluded its hunters.

The **Persephone's** midship house lived on. The forward section was salvaged, while the stern was left to haunt the deep.

About a year after the sinking, an Esso tanker, the **Livingston Roe**, suffered great damage to its midship house while it was moored at Recife, Brazil. The **Livingston Roe** was towed to Baltimore, where shipbuilders installed the midship house of the **Persephone** to what was left of the **Livingston Roe**. The grafted new ship went on to serve her masters well.

The tragedy of the **Persephone** was among those incidents along the American East Coast that have failed to spark the imagination of the American public as they may–and should–have.

Tons of shipping were destroyed by the German subs, within sight and even earshot of the beaches.

We know all too well of the war in distant places. But for the merchant vessels and crews that plied the coast in those troubled years, the fighting was right at their gangplanks.

Today, the stern section of the **Persephone** rests in about 50 feet of water, about 2.7 miles east of the North Monument.

The wreck is a favorite of area divers, and many an underwater explorer has become so engrossed by the magnitude of the remains, shattered into many scattered pieces, that they ascend to the surface some distance from their dive boat.

This silent, morbid World War II memorial to the nine men who were lost, and the ship that was destroyed, is not on an Italian beach, not on the cliffs of Normandy or the Lagoon of Truk.

It is but a thirty minute boat ride from Barnegat Inlet.

✡

COLLISION AT SEA

A dense fog blanketed the ocean surface on Wednesday, April 16, 1947 as the ocean-going tug **Great Isaac** and the Norwegian freighter **Bandeirante** headed on collision courses that led to the demise of the tug.

Bound from Norfolk to New York with the Liberty Ship **Thomas M. Cooley** in tow, the **Great Isaac** never made it to the piers of Gotham. After its encounter with the **Bandeirante**, the 1,117-ton seagoing beast of burden traveled only about 90 feet more–straight to the shifting sands below.

Today, the wreck of the **Great Isaac** is one of the more accessible and interesting of all the dive sites off Long Beach Island, resting on its side about six miles due east of Brant Beach.

Today, lobsters are plentiful on what is left of the tug's corpse. Encrusted with mussel growth, the wreck was stripped of its control room by salvagers years after its sinking.

The sinking of the **Great Isaac** was swift and certain, but thankfully, all crew members managed to escape serious injury.

As you will read later, however, there was a bizarre loss incurred by one of the crew men aboard the tug.

The **Great Isaac**, a Maritime Commission vessel under the Moran Towing and Transportation Company flag, was steaming through the thick mist, sounding its horn at regular, regulation intervals. Through the fog, the **Isaac's** skipper, Ernest McCreary, could hear the plaintive bleat of the freighter's horn.

As any sailor knows, a fogbound sea is at once treacherous and, in its way, the personification of the "romance of the deep." The throaty growl of a foghorn can play tricks on even the most seasoned seafaring lookout.

The sound dances, punches through the viscid vapor and unseen vessels manifest without warning.

Such was the case on that day in April, 1947, as the bow lookouts kept vigil aboard the **Great Isaac**. Cutting through the fog, the massive stem of the 3,806-ton, Cuba-bound freighter dwarfed the tug, slammed into it amidships and ripped six feet into the smaller ship's engine room.

It was the beginning of the end for the **Isaac**. That end, the 27 crew members of the tug found out, would come much too quickly. While all escaped with their lives, all lost their personal gear.

Crew member Vernie Cross, a 24-year old New Yorker, suffered perhaps the most serious bodily injury, a lacerated hand, while lowering a lifeboat.

Perhaps more serious than the loss of any sea bag contents, however, was the loss sustained by 59-year old Brooklynite Robert McCabe. McCabe watched with personal horror as a vital part of his very being dropped into the murky water and slithered to the bottom.

McCabe's loss?

His false teeth!

Sorting out the details of the collision, Leif Bjornstad, master of the **Bandeirante**, owned by the Fred Olsen Company of Oslo, said neither he nor any of his crew men heard any fog signals from the tug. He ordered full astern when the tug was spotted through the fog, but it was too late.

The freighter's bow was scarred by two gashes, but both were above the water line and posed no danger to the ship's seaworthiness.

The **Bandeirante** remained dead in the water as the **Great Isaac** slipped beneath the waves and her men hastened aboard the lifeboats.

Within a half hour, all survivors were safe aboard the freighter. Later, the tug **Trinidad Head** arrived at the scene to take the Liberty Ship under tow. The Bandeirante steamed toward a rendezvous with the repair dock.

If you're a diver and you venture on a course of 153 degrees to about ten miles from the North Monument, you'll be over the **Great Isaac**. You're liable to find its hulk, frozen in time, crawling with crustaceans and very inviting.

Oh yes, if you happen to rummage through the silt and sand of the ocean floor and find what may appear to be a most exotic form of marine life, beware!

It just might be Bob McCabe's long-lost dentures!

✡

The Sea King shortly after its 1963 beaching.

THE GHOSTLY MAST

At this writing, the only visible shipwreck on the beaches near Barnegat Inlet is a mere mast, jutting from the sand just off 10th Street in Barnegat Light.

For anyone caught up in the mystery of a shipwreck, this mast is a lure and a landmark signifying the ghostly relic to which it is attached. That relic, buried deeply in the sand, is the remains of the former fishing vessel, the **Sea King**.

The striking mast marks the grave of this ship which was beached in February, 1963.

For two decades, the ship has variously been underwater, under the sand, and high and dry on the beach.

Daring youngsters once crawled over the hulk when lifeguards' heads were turned, and even leaped into the sea from her mast.

Fishermen cherished the wreck when the water wrapped around her and she became a reef and thus home to many species of fish.

Her location made her attractive to shore fishermen who could cast to her edge and pluck the prized swimmers from the shallow water.

There is no apparent reason for the vessel to be where

76

she is today. She was a clamming boat bound from Staten Island, New York, to a southern port when she ran aground.

The day was described as cold but calm. The surface of the ocean was misty, and visibility was less than desirable. Those aboard doubtlessly knew of the perils of Barnegat Shoals, and should have known better than to venture too close to shore.

There are questions raised about the episode that led to the demise of the **Sea King**.

Was it true that the crew "whooped it up" a bit too much the night before she left port?

Was it true that the **Sea King** wasn't even outfitted with charts of the coast?

The **Sea King** was towing a former U.S. Government wooden-hulled minesweeper (below) to New York where it was to be refurbished and converted into a clamming vessel.

What should have been a routine voyage proved quite eventful when the **Sea King** brushed perilously close to the shore and eventually into the rocks of the south jetty of Barnegat Inlet.

The rugged rocks ripped through the clammer's prop, V-struts, shaft and rudder. The ship foundered, lacking any steering, and went aground just off the beach at 10th Street.

The minesweeper also washed ashore (photo below), but it was easily freed from the shallow bottom and pulled out of the area. The **Sea King** was a different story.

For a week, salvage crews struggled to free the **Sea King**. Bulldozers came to the scene and plowed into the sand as lines attached to the south jetty stabilized the ship.

Slowly, the glue-like sand released its prey. For a time, the ship was extricated and it appeared that she may be refloated. Gradually, however, the sand reclaimed the vessel and the salvage efforts were abandoned.

◻

THE STOLT DAGALI: SHEARED IN TWO

The North Atlantic some seventeen miles northeast of Barnegat Inlet was dismally dark, hauntingly quiet and choked by fog at 2:20 a.m., Thanksgiving Day, November 26, 1964.

Revelers aboard the six-month old Israeli Zim Lines flagship **Shalom** were partying into the wee small hours of the morning, oblivious to the threatening maritime weather that enveloped the giant luxury liner in a Stygian shroud.

Indeed, even when the stem of the liner sliced through the Norwegian tanker **Stolt Dagali**, few of the 616 passengers noticed much more than a split-second lurch and a sudden tinkling of ice cubes in their drink glasses.

For nineteen men aboard the tanker, however, that instant was to be the last of their lives.

The 583-foot, 12,723-ton tanker was gorged with solvents and fuel oil. She had set sail the previous day from Marcus Hook, Pennsylvania, and was bound for Newark, New Jersey before heading across the Atlantic to Rotterdam.

The late autumn seas had turned to a bitter 55 degrees and both ships steamed cautiously through the fog. Their radars were functional, but even those sophisticated electronic pathfinders can be victimized by the fury of the sea.

Somehow, neither ship's scopes showed the other's "blip," and with no warning, they collided.

The massive steel stem of the **Shalom** sliced through the 70-foot width of the **Stolt Dagali** with a deafening,

79

horrifying shriek. As a chain saw shears balsa, the liner sheared the tanker in half.

Of the 19 men of the **Stolt Dagali** who met their destinies, no doubt many were killed upon impact. They met their deaths instantly.

Others were trapped in the stern section of the **Stolt Dagali**, which sank quickly.

The bow of the tanker remained afloat after the collision, and still aboard that section were ten crew men and their master, Captain Kristean Bandersen. All were rescued. The bow section was towed to port. A new stern and engine room were crafted to it, and the ship was reborn with a new name.

Within an hour after the accident, rescue ships and helicopters scrambled to the scene. The **Stolt Dagali's** surviving crew men (and one woman) were taken aboard to safety, after many had fought valiantly in the bone-chilling waters as oil gushing from the tanker turned the waves into an unctuous brine.

Several were coated with a thick, all-engulfing layer of oil as they were saved.

It was a chaotic scene of tragedy in the darkness that morning. The shattered, forlorn severed hulk of the **Stolt Dagali's** bow floated tenuously as the majestic **Shalom** (with a 40-foot gash just above the waterline) stood by.

Various pieces of debris and flotsam marked the tomb of the tanker's aft section and the watery graves of 19 seamen.

When all was brought into some semblance of order, and there was nothing left for it to do, the Israeli passenger liner got underway for her berth in Manhattan.

Damage to the $20 million liner was assessed, and it was decided that the Newport News Shipbuilding Company could best do the necessary repairs and send the ship back to service out of her home port in Haiti.

The **Shalom** was back in service just before the new

year.

The stern section of the **Stolt Dagali** has remained on the ocean floor, resting on its side in about 120 feet of water.

Weekend scuba divers have taken ship's china and various pieces of hardware from her innards, easily accessible to all who care to venture into this grim metal mausoleum that serves as the final resting place for 19 sailors.

¤

SECOND EDITION

Addendum

•

"NEVER A NIGHT SO LONG"

Halloween night, 1890. The sky was clear and the sea was calm. And, while all appeared to hospitable for an uneventful night off Barnegat Inlet, 70 souls would perish in a collision which seemed to have no rhyme or reason.

The **Vizcaya** was a solid steamer built in the London yards of J.W. Dudgeon in 1872. Christened as the **Santander**, the 287-foot, 2,450-ton vessel was given her new name when purchased by the Compañia Transatlantica Española. That night in 1890, she was bound from New York to Cuba with breadstuffs, machinery, general merchandise, and 16 passengers.

The **Cornelius Hargraves** was a 1,332-ton, 211-foot four-masted schooner from the legendary shipyards of Camden, Maine. A double-decked coal carrier, she was bound from Philadelphia to Fall River, Mass. on October 31, 1890.

Those two ships, and those who commanded and crewed them, are the central figures in a baffling disaster that created nearly as much havoc later on land as it did at sea.

The masts of the **Hargraves** (or *Hargreaves*, in some accounts) towered over the low profile of the **Vizcaya**.

As the two ships approached under the moonless sky that fateful night, lookouts aboard each could make out the profiles of the other.

Felipe Hazas was chief officer of the steamer.

82

"The captain and the third officer were on the bridge at about 8:30," he told investigators, "and the steamer was making her way southward at a good pace. The weather was good and there was a light wind, but no fog.

"Suddenly through the darkness the ghostlike shadow of a big schooner's sails appeared on the starboard hand. She carried no lights, though ours were burning brightly. Before a thing could be done she had struck us a terrible blow just abaft the coal bunkers."

The **Vizcaya** was nearly sheared in two. The schooner reeled back from the wounded steamer and somehow rammed into it again. Lifeboats, rigging, and fittings on the **Vizcaya** were swept away by the bowsprit of the **Hargraves**. Within minutes, both ships were settling into the sands below.

"The crushing force of the schooner's blow carried her bow clean into the engine room," Hazas continued. "Water poured into our vessel in a torrent. It was evident that nothing could be done to save the ship, and two of the boats had been smashed to pieces. We succeeded in lowering a third, and one man got into it. Just as he was casting off the rails, the steamer sank."

A survivor later told a reporter, "Captain (Francisco) Cunill was on the bridge at the time, and was crushed by the schooner's bowsprit. The passengers were below in the saloon and smoking room and rushed on deck as soon as the shock was felt. Many people, crew and passengers, jumped aboard the schooner as she slid along after the second impact, thinking themselves safer there.

Some plunged into the frigid water to seek planks and spars as flotation devices. Others took to the masts and rigging.

Rescue crews were told that some 20 men clambered into the rigging. A contemporary newspaper account told of their fate.

"The poor fellows, used to southern suns, could not

stand the penetrating cold of the long, dark night, and dropped exhausted, one by one, into the sea."

Felipe Hazas was one who survived.

"The cold and wet were almost unbearable," he said. "And never was the night so long."

The salvation of the survivors of the **Vizcaya**-**Hargraves** collision came when the Brazilian steamer **Humboldt** came upon the scene after the next day's dawn had broken.

A lookout on the **Humboldt** spotted a set of masts protruding above the waves some six miles off Barnegat. From those masts he heard a cry for help.

As the **Humboldt** steered to the pitiful sight, a dozen ragged and near-frozen men were counted in the rigging.

As these survivors were hastened below for blankets and coffee, the **Humboldt** searched the wreckage for any other survivors—or victims. None were found.

By mid-morning, the **Humboldt** was at the foot of Jay Street in Brooklyn, and the investigation into the bizarre collision was underway.

That morning, the captain of the Barnegat Life-Saving Station had spotted the wreckage through a powerful telescope. As far south as Lewes, Delaware, survivors and bodies were taken ashore by passing vessels.

The disaster caused quite a stir in the shipping offices and courtrooms. Rumors of prominent people who died in the crash, and charges of cowardice on the part of the schooner's captain kept headline writers busy for weeks.

Indeed, the **Vizcaya** was carrying some interesting people.

Aboard was Juan Pedro, one of the richest sugar growers in Cuba. A millionaire many times over, Pedro was part owner of the shipping line which owned the steamer.

Ramon Alvarez, another **Vizcaya** passenger, was one of the most respected (and prosperous) cigar manufacturers of Havana.

SHIPWRECKS NEAR BARNEGAT INLET

And, the ship's captain, Francisco Cunill, was not only a ship's captain, but also a respected expert in naval construction. He, and the other officers of the **Vizcaya**, were members of the Spanish Royal Naval Reserve.

It was the captain of the **Hargraves**, however, who lived to tell of the incident–and answer charges of cowardice.

As a sailing vessel, the **Hargraves** had the right-of-way that night, and of that there was no doubt. Still, there were those on board both ships who claimed that once its officers spotted the steamer, the **Hargraves** could have made a course change to keep its distance.

Hindsight being "20/20", the rules of the nautical road went for naught that night.

"The collision was one of those things for which there was no reason and can be no excuse."

The words were those of Capt. John F. Allen, owner and master of the **Hargraves**.

He continued: "The **Hargraves** was undoubtedly upon her own course, with the right of way assured to her. It was not her place to get out of the way of the steamer. It was the steamer's duty to keep out of our way, and this is what she failed to do. She either did not or would not see us, and the crash was the result.

"From my knowledge of the rules of the sea and my own observation, I am satisfied as I am of my own existence that the neglect was theirs."

Capt. Allen's tone turned sour as he continued. "The steamer was first seen when we were five miles away, and the fellow who calls himself 'second mate' was in charge of the deck at the time. I was called soon after, and ran up half dressed and shoeless to find a steamer bearing down upon us."

That "fellow who calls himself 'second mate'" was Angus Walker, a Bostonian who leveled a hefty charge against his captain.

Walker claimed that he urged the captain to change

course, but the skipper remained steadfast. Furthermore, Walker said that Capt. Allen commandeered a lifeboat just after the collision. That lifeboat, said Walker, could have easily accommodated a dozen men, but the captain and three officers made haste from their sinking ship in an effort to save themselves.

Walker claimed that he climbed into the rigging and called out for the captain not to desert him and the other stranded crewmen. He said the captain did not reply, and rowed to safety.

"I knew the coward had made off," Walker said, "leaving the rest of the crew to perish miserably."

Back in Fall River, most folks in and out of the shipping offices found Walker's story hard to believe.

Capt. Allen vehemently denied the allegations.

"There is not a scintilla of truth in it," he shot back at a newspaper reporter who related Walker's tale of abandonment.

"Well, all that need saying about that officially," he said, "is that he (Walker) was left on board through his own negligence. When it was seen that we were about to sink, my chief officer ordered Walker to see to and take care of the boat and to keep it from being crowded down by the Spaniards, who were jumping aboard of us. Of course I should have been glad to save everybody if that had been possible, but it was not, and for a choice I gave my own men the first chance of saving themselves. And that they were saved is the best proof that I was alive to their needs and looking after their lives."

Capt. Allen continued. "When I left the **Hargraves** I supposed that we had got all our men in the boat. I knew the boat was full, but it was so dark I could not distinguish who were in it. What had become of Walker and where he had gone when, cur-like, he deserted his duty, I do not know. He ought to have been with us, and it was his own fault that he was not, and the one mystery I cannot solve is why he stole away from his post of duty.

"Desert him? No sir!"

After the charges and countercharges subsided, and the list of survivors was checked against the number of passengers and crew on both vessels, it was determined that 70 men, women, and children died as the result of the strange collision that night.

The **Vizcaya** remains a part of local lore around Barnegat Inlet. Fishermen and divers call it "The Spanish Wreck," and it is a favorite target for their exploits. The remains of the **Hargraves** rest on the sea bottom about two miles from the **Vizcaya**.

•

THE CHRISTMAS STORM OF '09

Death takes no holiday at sea. In 1908, a coastal storm killed 11 people along the New Jersey shore during the Christmas holidays.

Off Barnegat Inlet, the schooner barge **Gwennie** went down with five lives—one of many such cargo gorged maritime workhorses to break from their tows in strong weather.

The following year, fierce weather over the holiday season claimed more property and lives.

From the Delaware River to the bays and beyond, South Jersey was beaten severely by wind and wet snow. Roofs were ripped from hotels in Asbury Park, while telegraph and rail service was disrupted to the point that several seaside resorts—Atlantic City among them—were completely isolated from the rest of the world for several hours.

In Atlantic City, a weather observer recorded the lowest barometer reading in the history of the town.

Several inches of snow blanketed Philadelphia and points inland, while the shore experienced only a coating. Most precipitation there was a wet snow which melted on contact with land. Still, Barnegat Bay was frozen over, and gales swept across the Atlantic.

The night after Christmas, 1909, distress signals were noticed on shore north of Barnegat Inlet. Soon, the wireless buzzed with a message from the steamer **S.S. Thurman**. She, her cargo of bituminous coal, and her crew of 22 had washed ashore.

The Standard Oil coaster had been towing three barges, which were also carrying soft coal. The third in the tow line was crewed by five men. In the midst of the raging storm, the hawser snapped and cast that third barge adrift.

In a noble attempt to rescue those aboard the barges, the **Thurman** herself was blasted by the blinding winds. For two hours, the ship steamed in search of the wayward barge, but to no avail. And, it was during this search that the Thurman was shoved onto a sandbar.

The storm threatened to crush the vessel and doom its crew. In response to the distress flares from the **Thurman**, Life-Saving crews responded with breeches buoy and cannon.

Capt. Jeremiah Hardap was the last to be saved from the whaleback steamer, which had been built for duty on the Great Lakes.

Plunged deeply bow-first into the bar, the **Thurman** was battered by the pounding surf until she broke in two amidships.

Salvagers had their way with what was left of the wreck, while those crew members who were set adrift on the ill-fated barge were never heard from again.

•

THE SEA RAIDERS

The carnage at the hands of German torpedoes in the spring of 1918 has been detailed elsewhere in this volume and in the companion book, *Shipwrecks Off Ocean City*.

The Kaiser's U-Boats, called by some headline writers

and historians, "Sea Raiders," exacted their tolls of lives and cargo in short, swift and savage attacks along an American coast caught totally unaware and unprotected.

By mid-June, 1918, a makeshift fleet of coastal defense boats was mobilized by the Navy Department, and the troop carriers and supply ships which plied the sea off New Jersey were afforded some protection.

It is interesting to note, however, that as the country licked its maritime wounds and applied a military bandage on the shipping lanes, investigators worked diligently on shore to ferret out suspected spies.

From Lewes, Delaware, to Long Beach Island and north, rumors were rampant about bands of German sympathizers who led the "pirate submarines" to their prey.

"Mysterious flashes of light" along certain shore points were believed to be signals from the bands of traitors.

And, while little was ever confirmed (or, at least, reported to the public) by the Secret Service and other organizations, it was believed that the U-Boats' actions were aided by what one report called "A treason band, directed by a mysterious woman—a woman of keen mind and high intelligence" who was furnishing the raiders via "a carefully concealed wireless station and a system of light signals in code."

•

STEERING TO DEATH

It was shortly after nine o'clock, January 24, 1935. The night was bitterly cold—five degrees above zero, by one account.

The **S.S. Mohawk** was southbound on a course for Cuba. The ten-year old steel liner, more than 400 feet long and carrying 54 passengers and a crew of 109, was clipping along toward Barnegat Inlet at about 15 knots.

That heady speed may not have been in the best interest of all involved, since the **Mohawk**'s automatic steering device was disabled, and the vessel was being steered from the engine room.

George Clancy, a lookout on the **Mohawk**'s bow that night, said he definitely saw what was coming, and what would lead to the demise of the Ward Line steamer.

What he saw was the big Norwegian freighter, the **Talisman**.

Due for a call in Claymont, Del., the **Talisman** was about an eighth of a mile from the **Mohawk**, and about to be passed by the single-stack steamer.

"Our steering gear gave way," Clancy said later, "and Captain Wood, seeing that an accident could not be helped, blew a loud blast of his whistle as a warning to the **Talisman** to keep to port.

"A few minutes later the **Talisman** struck the port bow of the **Mohawk**, opening a big hole in her side. Water poured in. The bow of the **Talisman** went through the forecastle. There were a number of sailors in there at the time and I'm afraid some of them must have been killed."

After the collision, the **Mohawk**'s skipper attempted to turn his ship toward shallow water and a better chance of survival.

As the sea poured into the gash on the **Mohawk**'s port side, the big ship listed to port, and then to starboard, and then plunged bow-first, 72 feet beneath the waves.

With it went the lives of 16 passengers and 30 crew members.

Robert Barnett was a seaman on the bridge of the **Mohawk** that night.

"The ship's telemotor went haywire," he told an investigator. "The **Mohawk** immediately swung hard over to port and then men were sent below to connect the hand steering apparatus. The crash came before this could be done."

•

WRECKS BY DESIGN

In 1935, several fishermen from the Cape May and Wildwood areas watched as several boats sank some ten miles off the shoreline.

They watched with a certain anticipation, as the intentional sinking of the vessels and other assorted claptrap was the planting of the seed which would become the Jersey shore's first artificial reef or, as it would be called, "fish haven."

Since then, several artificial reefs have been created along the coast. Leavings from construction jobs (what was carved from below the streets of New York during subway construction is now part of a "fish haven") and everything from old cars, surplus government materiel and decommissioned ships, even used roadway slabs from the Ben Franklin Bridge in Philadelphia, have gone to the bottom.

Working with fishery and environmental experts, and the U.S. Army Corps of Engineers, the artificial reef builders have created myriad mounds around which fish feed and breed.

It is interesting to note that in addition to the random rubble, some interesting vessels have been towed to their grave sites, blasted under supervision by the U.S. Coast Guard and other authorities, and sent to the sand.

The closest artificial reef to Barnegat Inlet, and a favorite of local anglers, is the Garden State North Reef.

Five hundred bundled tires, a pilot house, a 250-foot molasses barge and a 110-foot supply barge are among the pieces of wreckage which comprise the reef, which was begun in 1984.

But, the most recognizable name of the vessels of the reef is none other than the **Queen Mary**.

No, not *that* **Queen Mary**, of course. The **Queen**

Mary which lies at the bottom some seven miles south-southeast from Barnegat Inlet was a 31-foot cabin cruiser. And, it is the smallest of the ships and boats of the "fish haven."

The **Good Times**, a 52-foot wooden-hulled charter boat, was the first vessel to be dropped. It was joined later by the 85-foot barge, the **Shirley Ann**.

The largest ships of Garden State North are the **A.H. Dumont**, a 247-foot tanker, and the **Fatuk**.

The **Fatuk** has an interesting history. When sunk on October 27, 1986, the vessel was only 23 years old. Built in Tokushuma Zonsen Sangyo, Japan, the refrigerated freighter was designed to carry fish.

For many years, it served the Japanese fishing industry until in 1985, the U.S. Customs Service discovered its cargo gave new meaning to "reefer."

Laden with marijuana its crew was attempting to smuggle into a New England port, the ship was confiscated and ordered destroyed.

The **Fatuk** was towed to its destiny, its sea cocks were opened, and the vessel went down intact.

Sea bass, porgy, and blackfish congregate around the **Fatuk** and the other outcasts in the undersea oasis of Garden State North.

They are joined by ling, pollock, cod, and the occasional shark and bluefish. The lobster catch has been termed good, as well.

The smugglers' loss has been the anglers' gain.

●●●